Co

MW01107470

P. M. Batty

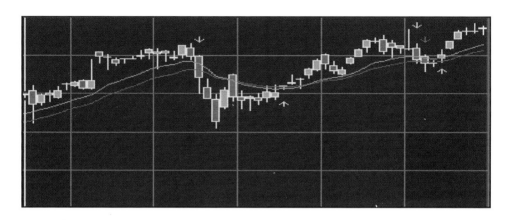

Learn how to trade covered calls
in well illustrated easy-to-follow steps

Stock	Stock Price	Option	Exp. Month	Strike	P/C	Last Trade	Static % Return
VRTX	29.28	VQRDF	April	30	C	2.88	10.77%

Buy the stock (VRTX) for $29.28	Sell the April 30c option contract)	Option expires in April (3rd Friday)	Market buys stock from you automatically if the stock goes above $30.00	Receive $2.88 for the option premium (10.77%)

Turbo Trainer
Mission Statement

Teach Stock Market Strategies
Quickly
Effectively
Inexpensively

Books in the Turbo Trainer Series

Covered Calls
Consistent Cash Flow

Calls and Puts
Fast Horses, Steel Nerves,
Quick Money

Six Effective Charting Techniques
Roadmap for Making Money

Candlesticks
10 Patterns to Make Money
390 not to Bother With

3-Day Investment Strategies
Get In, , Make Money, Get Out
Or Stay in and Die

Credit Spreads
Make Money When Stocks
do not Move

10 Investment Mistakes In the Market
Avoid Them and Win

Mini-Futures and the FOREX
What the Other Guys are
Doing Who Already
Know the Stock Market

Covered calls may well be the safest play in the market. A stock can only move in three directions, up, down or sideways.
Covered calls make money for the investor in two of these three directions.
There is an additional benefit. Covered calls teach patience and tend to mute the greed-need lurking inside all of us.

P. M. Batty

An apology

Often throughout this book, principles of trading, trading rules, concepts and theories are repeated.

I am aware of that. I am also aware that if I make the assumption that everything anyone reads for the first time will be immediately absorbed, that is probably naïve on my part.

So when I talk about a trading principle using concepts previously explained I sometimes repeat the concept. This prevents you having to leaf backward to review and perhaps lose the momentum of the idea I'm presenting.

I apologize for the repetition. I hope it is more helpful than irritating.

Contents

Preface

Trading covered calls involves two steps. The first is buying stock. Ideally, I seek to buy a stock that is in a trading range (going sideways or sometimes called basing), or trending slightly upward. Once I've isolated and purchased a stock (at least 100 shares) that I believe, demonstrates 30-60 days of a predictable trend, I then execute the second step. I sell an option on my stock position. I'm offering my stock for sale...for more than I paid for it.

I will concede that there is that there is a possibility that the stock will "shoot through the roof" and I will not make as much money as if I just owned the stock. I'll explain the specifics of that circumstance later. The fact still remains that if I just own stock, I can make money only if the stock goes up in value (dividends not withstanding). With covered calls, I can make money in two directions; up and sideways.

To reiterate: Except for stocks paying dividends, a stock has to increase in price and you have to sell it to make money. With covered calls, the stock can be in a sideways trend until you grow a grey beard to your belt and you can make money selling options on it every month while still owning the stock.

Chapter 1
Trading tools...the three most important ones

The age of electronics has given the average trader almost unlimited availability to methods to trade the stock market. Indeed, we can all drown in research.

The real challenge has not been to learn about all these tools. Rather the challenge has been which tools to eliminate.

The truth is that there is no set method for every trade. Each strategy lends itself to a specific search for stocks with patterns matching the search.

Three tools that do have a universal application are:

1. <u>A search engine:</u> Something electronic or written (news paper) that finds stocks with a specific set of behaviors conducive to successful trades.

2. <u>A charting program:</u> Charts are a historical representation of how a stock has performed and illustrate patterns which suggest future performance. Most charting programs come with a news link providing:
   a. General news
   b. Earnings announcement dates

3. <u>A broker account to make the trade:</u> The best broker is one that works best for you. There are over 900 from which to choose.

Fortunately there are many search engines for covered calls, and charts that reveal stocks with good patterns for trading them. There are also brokers who have trade tickets designed especially for covered calls.

Further it is comforting to know that the trading industry, for the most part, considers covered calls as one of the most consistent money makers in the market.

•This strategy combines the stability of a stock trade with the dynamics of an option trade.

•Essentially, it is possible to
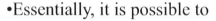
–Make money when the stock rises in price
–Make money when the stock stays flat
–Reduce the loss when the stock falls in price

•All other things being equal, there are 2 out of 3 chances for a winning trade.

•With an informed approach, you can increase the odds even more.

•Note: When I talk about a rate of return I'm talking about a monthly rate of return. If I can get a 3% rate of return, that's 36% annualized.

•If you follow the principles in the book, while I make no guarantee, a 3% rate of return per month is very conservative.

Why trade covered calls?

I've been teaching workshops on the stock market for the past 10 years. I've taught for other companies and sponsored my own. One problem the stock market presents is how to teach the various elements of trading which seem so disjointed. How does someone who would like to know more about the market stay interested when they're dropped in a sea of new language and new concepts?

The solution which has emerged seems too easy. Most of us are interested if we have an idea how much money we might be able to make with a certain strategy. Then we will work toward learning the rationale behind it.

So here it is: You can make from 3% to 12% per month (36%-144% per year) on covered calls. If that interests you, this book is worth the read.

Below is an "ink-wet" quote. Said differently, a quote that was current at the time of this writing. This is somewhat atypical in that it is a huge rate of return (13%). Normally, premiums are not this high. Even so, it starts the blood running just a little faster. I could make this trade and it could go south It could maintain a price at or around $34.08 (its current price) or it could continue its trend to the upside. As illustrated on the previous page, if it stays flat or goes up I make money. I've a

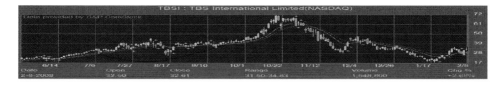

Date	Stock Symbol	Stock Price	Option	Bid Premium	% Rate of Return	Annualized % Return
11-Feb-08	TBSI	34.08	Mar 35c	4.4	13%	135%

two-out-of-three chance of making a winning trade, all other things being equal.

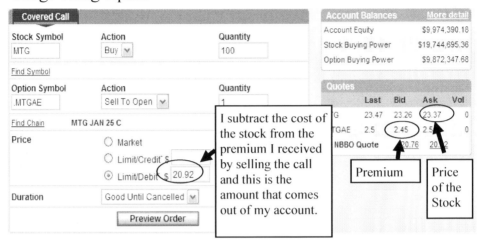

Mechanics of the Covered Call Strategy

In the stock market there have to be buyers and sellers, or the whole market falls apart. With covered calls I am both a buyer and seller. I buy a stock (I am the buyer) and I sell an option (I am the seller). The order ticket illustrated is an example of a trade. I paid $23.37 for a stock. I can sell the market the right to buy my stock at $25.00. For that right, I'm paid a premium. In this example $2.45. Again, I sell an option. The option, in this case is called a "call". When I sell a call, someone has the right to "call" my stock away from me. My call option has a short life. I can sell a standard call option that lasts up to 8 months in the future. However, with covered calls, I sell a call that has one or two months' worth of time. As a general rule, calls expire the 3rd Friday of the month. Technically, options expire on noon the Saturday following the 3rd Friday, but the public can't trade on Saturday so for me, the option expires on market close, on the 3rd Friday.

Assume it is December 22nd. The 3rd Friday in December has come and gone. If I buy a stock for $23.37 and sell the market the right to buy my stock away from me for $25.00, the call that I sell is a January Call. As stated above, I could sell a February or a March etc. but the covered call strategy usually only sells calls for the next month out because it's more profitable to do it that way. Because I sold the January Call, I have to hold my stock until the 3rd Friday of January. Indeed, the broker won't let me sell my stock before that date because his trading program sees that I own a stock and I have promised to hold it through the 3rd Friday. As long as that call exists, I cannot sell my stock. There are exceptions, but we'll stay with the simple approach for now.

Here's the great news. I charge the market a fee when I agree *not* to sell my stock. The fee is called a premium. Premiums for call options are found in a call option table or chain.

As you can see on the previous page, the premium I received (found in an option table) is $2.45. $2.45/23.37 = 10.48\%$

Those familiar with real estate will see that this is very similar to a lease-to-own contract. I own a house and I lease it to someone, usually for a year. For one year, they have a right to buy the house at a fixed price. If they don't buy the house by the end of the year, their lease expires. I can lease it to someone else, I keep the lease money, of course, and I still own the house. The stock market works the same way...just more quickly.

If my stock goes up in value...say $28.00, the market will buy my stock from me. Except in rare circumstances the market buys my stock away from me when the option expires, not before. But they only pay me $25.00 because I agreed to sell it for that amount. Still I bought it for $23.37 and sold it for $25.00 and also kept a $2.45 premium. So I made $1.63 on the sale of the stock, and $2.45 on the premium. That's $4.08

in 30 days on a $23.37 investment. $4.08/$23.37 = 17.45% for one month. There are commissions to pay, and they must be taken into consideration. However since they vary from roughly $2.00 to $25.00 depending on which broker I use, they are not included in the profit calculation. I realize that I could have made $5.00 by just buying the stock and selling it. However, I did not know that the stock was going to go up that much.

What if the stock stayed below $25.00, say $24.75? No one is going to buy my stock away from me for $25.00 if it's only worth $24.75. On the 3rd Friday of January, the call option expires. I get to keep the $2.45 premium (I keep the premium regardless of what happens to the stock). I did not sell my stock and I still made $2.45. What do you think I'm going to do for February? Right! I'm going to sell another call if I still like the stock.

What if the stock falls in value? It can go to 20.92 before I lose any money. As long as it stays in a trading range of somewhere between $22.00 and $25.00, I'm going to continue to sell calls on it.

As stated earlier, with covered calls, if the stock goes up, I make money. If the stock stays flat, I make money. If the stock falls, the premium that I made selling a call option on my stock reduces the loss.

The disadvantage of covered calls is that I cap my profit. I once bought the stock Sepracor, symbol SEPR. I paid $28.00 and change for it. I sold the $30 strike price call for $2.00 and change. The next day SEPR went to $41.00. Was I happy? Yep.

I made roughly $4.00 on SEPR. That's 16.6% for one month. It was a covered call strategy. That's how I designed it. My

Shudda, cudda, wudda is a game for dummies. Stick with thoughtso, didit, yeeha.. The "yeeha" at the end means the trade was a success.

Covered calls gives me constant cash flow

Now I've illustrated a covered call trade. On the previous example, if the stock does not go down in price, I will have made just over 10%.

The problem with trading the market is that it is unpredictable. Covered calls help increase market predictability by using semi-volatile stocks as a basis instead of more volatile, less predictable stocks.

By selling premiums each month on stocks I own, I generate positive cash flow...barring, of course, a fall in the price of the stock. Indeed, the entire concept of covered calls is based on owning a semi-volatile stock…and then SELLING the market the right (a call option) to buy my stock away from me.

By selling calls on my stock each month, I generate constant cash flow on a monthly basis whether I sell my stock or not.

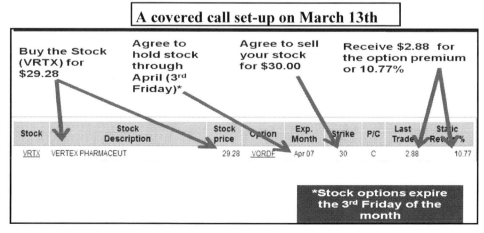

A covered call set-up on March 13th

	Buy the Stock (VRTX) for $29.28	Agree to hold stock through April (3rd Friday)*	Agree to sell your stock for $30.00	Receive $2.88 for the option premium or 10.77%

Stock	Stock Description	Stock price	Option	Exp. Month	Strike	P/C	Last Trade	Static Return %
VRTX	VERTEX PHARMACEUT	29.28	VQRDF	Apr 07	30	C	2.88	10.77

*Stock options expire the 3rd Friday of the month

What is a strike price ?

Basically, an option is a contract to sell my stock (in the case of covered calls).

I have to agree with the market as to what price I'm willing to sell...I strike a price.

To maintain some modicum of sanity, strike prices are fixed. This prevents me from offering to sell my stock at an arbitrary number and causing an accounting nightmare. Strike prices are usually in $2.50 increments for stocks under $25.00, $5.00 increments, for stocks between $25.00 and $200.00 and $10.00 increments for stocks over $200

Later, I'll tie strike prices into my trading strategy. But for now, I'll stick with the definition that a strike price is the price at which I'm willing to sell my stock.

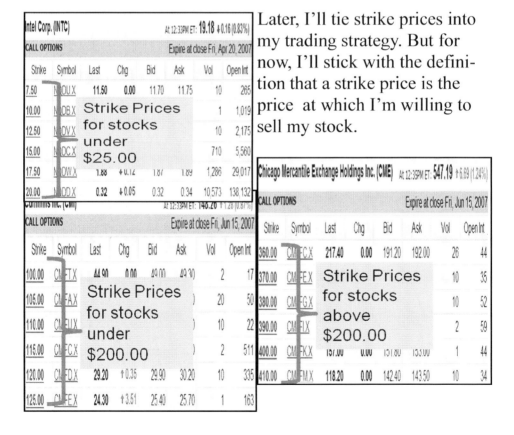

Disadvantage of Covered Calls illustrated

Every strategy in the market has advantages and disadvantages. The covered call strategy is no different. When I buy a stock and agree to sell it to the market for more than I paid for it (a strike price) the market believes the stock will go higher than my strike price. I agree to make it available to the market for a specific price for a specific time. Since I "freeze my asset" for a fixed period, the market pays a premium for the time I agree to keep your stock available to the market. If the stock goes above the value of the strike price, the market will pay me the value of the strike price, but no more. Therefore, I "cap my profit".

The amount I make on a covered call is always limited. That's the disadvantage. However, if I'm making 5% a month (very possible) that's about 60% a year simple interest…not a bad rate of return.

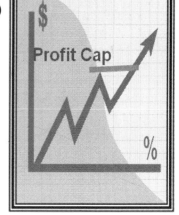

Example:

I buy a stock for $29.00
I strike a price at which the market has the right to buy your stock from you. In this example let's say $30.00.
I sell the market the right to take the stock at $30.00. I receive a premium of say $1.50 (About 5%...1.50/29.00 = 5.2%). If the stock goes to $35.00, the market will take my stock and pay me $30.00. Although I receive $1.00 more for the stock than I paid for it, I are not paid the present value of the stock ($35.00) because I agreed to sell it for $30.00.

Who takes the other side of the trade?

I stated before that the covered call strategy is one in which I can

>   –make money when the stock goes up
>   –make money when the stock goes sideways
>   –reduce or, in some cases, eliminate my loss when the
>   stock falls in value.

Along about now, you've got to be asking yourself:

>   –Who takes the other side of the trade?
>   –It's a legitimate question. Am I building a strategy that I   can't sell?

Actually, I don't have to worry who is going to take the other side of the trade and I don't really care. Barring a huge catastrophe I can rest assured that:

-The market is liquid.
-If the market offers this opportunity, and has done so for the past 30 years, that's good news.
-I don't have to worry that something the market has been doing for 30 years suddenly won't work for me.

When I persisted with these types of questions early on in my trading career, my mentor, after much long suffering shouted: **"It will work. Just make the trade".**

WARNING and Disclaimer!

Trading Options is not for everyone.

Before trading options, a copy of "Characteristics and Risks of Standardized Options" should be obtained from your Broker and read.

It is possible to lose your entire trading portfolio (all your money) in option trading.

Author's note: I know of no living person who's read this small book cover to cover.

•There are no recommendations or guarantees, written or implied, regarding investments or trading.

◦This material is instructional in nature only.

CHARACTERISTICS AND RISKS OF STANDARDIZED OPTIONS

February 1994
1995 through 2000
Supplements included

◦Specific investment advise is better left to financial advisors, not me or your brother-in-law (unless he's a financial advisor).

•Individual results from making trades may differ considerably from the illustrations in this book.

First things first

To understand the market we must first learn pieces of seemingly unconnected information.

For anyone trying to grasp the entire concept of covered calls without a basic understanding of how the market works, it can be extremely frustrating.

Our approach is to teach:

1. An overall concept of covered calls to include

    •Buying stocks
    •Selling Options

2. Simple methods to select which stock to buy and which option to sell.

3. Finally I'll illustrate trades using actual broker tickets and go step-by-step through simulated trades. Along the way I'll include the jargon of the market and what it means.

A note about simulated or paper trading. Often I hear that it does no good to paper trade because I sidestep the emotion of trading actual dollars. To those that harbor this belief, I'd like to be there when that theory is presented to a professional sports team...maybe the New England Patriots? I would pay big money to be there when someone tells Coach Belicheck he doesn't have to practice during the week because there are no crowds, no opposing team and no TV cameras. Paper trading is very effective if I keep track of my successes and failures. Otherwise, I agree with those who say it is a waste of time. So keep track of your money and don't trade the real stuff until you have recorded proof that you can do well trading the white stuff.

Chapter 2
Option basics

Any covered call trade requires a basic understanding of options.

•This next section discusses

–Option tables

–In, at and out of the money

–Time decay

–Which option to **SELL** in a covered call strategy.

Please note: In a covered call play, I am *selling* the call option. Many traders forget that they are the seller of the option, and they execute an order to buy options. It takes them totally outside the covered call strategy and does not generate constant cash flow...unless, of course, they are very lucky.

Options

Get Option

View By Expiration. **Mar 07** | Apr 07 | Jul 07 | Jan 08 | Jan 09

CALL OPTIONS						Expire at close Fri, Mar 16, 2007	
Strike	Symbol	Last	Chg	Bid	Ask	Vol	Open Int
27.50	SQXCY X	3.30	↓0.50	2.75	2.90	28	370
30.00	SQXCF X	0.60	↓0.35	0.55	0.60	675	4,096
32.50	SQXCZ X	0.05	↓0.05	NA	0.05	246	9,362
35.00	SQXCG X	0.05	0.00	NA	0.05	645	12,911
37.50	SQXCU X	0.05	0.00	NA	0.05	5	3,473
40.00	SQXCH X	0.05	0.00	NA	0.05	2	636
42.50	SQXCV X	0.05	0.00	NA	0.05	12	22

This is a picture of a partial option table. We will discuss each element of the complete table as we advance through the book.

Since I am buying a stock and selling an option, guidelines for both must be established.

What is an option?

•An option is a contract.

–It is the right or obligation

–To buy or sell a stock

–On or before a specific date

–At a specific (strike) price

•And, if we sell the call, on a stock we own, we receive a premium ($2.80 in the example below).

NOTE: An option contract holds 100 shares of stock. You cannot buy ½ contract. When calculating the price of a contract, you have to multiply the price of the premium x 100. For example: If an option sells for $2.80 (below) we multiply the $2.80 x 100. The option contract generates $280.00. Also, you must sell in increments of 1. You can, of course sell 2 or more. But you must have 100 shares of stock for each contract.. If you are in a position to sell in lots of 1,000 contracts, I'd love to take you to lunch and discuss a joint publication of my next book.

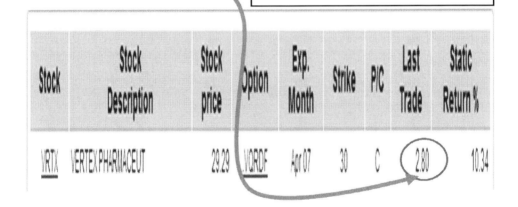

Stock	Stock Description	Stock price	Option	Exp. Month	Strike	P/C	Last Trade	Static Return %
VRTX	VERTEX PHARMACEUT	29.29	VQRDF	Apr 07	30	C	2.80	10.34

In English: 1. We buy a stock @ $29.29
2. We sell the market the right to buy our stock for $30.00 (the strike price)
3. We agree to hold our stock through the month of April (the current date is March 30th).
4. The market pays us a premium for buying the stock using our own money and making it available for a price of $30.00.
5. The Premium is $2.80

Options expire

If I sell an option for the month of April, it expires the Saturday following the third Friday of April.
Since I can't trade on Saturday, my option expires on the 3rd Friday of the month

The more time I sell, the more money I receive. BUT…I have to hold my stock for a longer period if I sell more time.
If I sell the February calls, I have to hold my stock through the 3rd Friday of February. If I sell the March calls, I have to hold my stock through the 3rd Friday of March and so on.

2007 Stock Options Expiration Calendar

Select a year: 2007

January	February	March
S M T W T F S	S M T W T F S	S M T W T F S
1 2 3 4 5 6	1 2 3	1 2 3
7 8 9 10 11 12 13	4 5 6 7 8 9 10	4 5 6 7 8 9 10
14 15 16 17 18 19 20	11 12 13 14 15 16 17	11 12 13 14 15 16 17
21 22 23 24 25 26 27	18 19 20 21 22 23 24	18 19 20 21 22 23 24
28 29 30 31	25 26 27 28	25 26 27 28 29 30 31

April	May	June
S M T W T F S	S M T W T F S	S M T W T F S
1 2 3 4 5 6 7	1 2 3 4 5	1 2
8 9 10 11 12 13 14	6 7 8 9 10 11 12	3 4 5 6 7 8 9
15 16 17 18 19 20 21	13 14 15 16 17 18 19	10 11 12 13 14 15 16
22 23 24 25 26 27 28	20 21 22 23 24 25 26	17 18 19 20 21 22 23
29 30	27 28 29 30 31	24 25 26 27 28 29 30

Generally, I look to sell the current month. It is better to get 5% for March and when March options expire, sell the April options for 5%. If I just sell the April options I probably will not get 10% right now. I'll probably only get about 6%.

Hypothetical Example:
A stock costs $19.00
Sell the March 20 calls for $1.00. $1.00/19.00 = 5.2%
When March expires, sell the April 20 calls for $1.00. Receive the same rate of return: 5.2%.
Total rate of return for 2 months = 10.4%

Or, only sell the April 20 Calls for $1.50. $1.50/$19.00 = 7.8%
Total rate of return for 2 months = 7.8%
Note: I made up the prices of the stock and the options. Actual prices are found in the stock charts and option tables. Option prices differ from month to month. So you won't get the same return each month, but usually it's in the ball park, assuming all other elements which affect an option price to have remained equal.

Also: Options have names: A March 20 Call means the option expires in March. "20" is the strike price. It's what your willing to sell your stock for. And a call is the type of option you're selling (as opposed to a put option).

Options are not available for every stock

There are, roughly 12,500 different companies that sell stock on the open market (called equities).
Of those 12,500, approximately 3,000 of them have options.
I do not know of one person who carries a list to keep track.

Here's an easier way to determine if a stock has options. Go to any options website like finance.yahoo.com (do not type www in the address field). Enter the symbol for the stock in question
Data about the stock is displayed
Click on Options

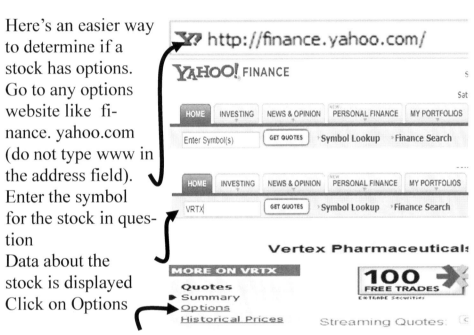

This is the options table that appears. It shows the options available for VRTX for December. Do not be overwhelmed by all the numbers. There are only a few key figures that we use. When we understand what they are, the option table becomes

View By Expiration: **Dec 07** | Jan 08 | Apr 08 | Jul 08 | Jan 09 | Jan 10

CALL OPTIONS					Expire at close Fri, Dec 21, 2007		
Strike	Symbol	Last	Chg	Bid	Ask	Vol	Open Int
17.50	VQRLW.X	8.40	0.00	7.90	8.20	4	4
20.00	VQRLD.X	5.50	0.00	5.40	5.70	10	34
22.50	VQRLX.X	3.50	0.00	3.20	3.40	20	244
25.00	VQRLE.X	1.15	↑ 0.05	1.10	1.25	43	1,490
30.00	VQRLF.X	0.10	0.00	N/A	0.10	10	5,483
35.00	VQRLG.X	0.10	0.00	N/A	0.05	30	2,318
40.00	VQRLH.X	0.05	0.00	N/A	0.05	6	166

The Options Table

•Since an option table comes up for VRTX, I can assume the stock has options…brilliant.

Whenever I look at an options table, the first thing I find is the **price of the stock**.

•**STEP #1:** If I were trading covered calls, I'd **buy** 100 shares of the stock at $29.29.

•**STEP #2:** and **sell** the April 30c (Described as the April 30 Calls) for 2.80.

As stated earlier, I sell the current month and one strike price out of the money (one strike price greater than the price of the stock).

Because an option contract controls 100 shares of stock, I must own stock in lots of 100. So the final trade would cost (without commissions) $29.29 x 100 = $2929.00.

The sale of the option contract brings $2.80 x 100 or $280 into my brokerage account the next day following the option sale.

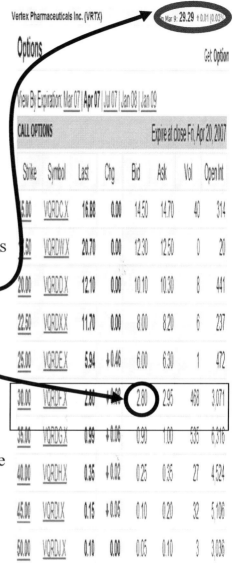

Vertex Pharmaceuticals Inc. (VRTX)

Mar 9: 29.29 +0.01 (0.03%)

Options   Get Option

View By Expiration: Mar 07 | Apr 07 | Jul 07 | Jan 08 | Jan 09

CALL OPTIONS							Expire at close Fri, Apr 20, 2007
Strike	Symbol	Last	Chg	Bid	Ask	Vol	Open Int
5.00	VQRDC.X	16.88	0.00	14.50	14.70	40	314
17.50	VQRDW.X	20.70	0.00	12.30	12.50	0	20
20.00	VQRDD.X	12.10	0.00	10.10	10.30	8	441
22.50	VQRDX.X	11.70	0.00	8.00	8.20	6	237
25.00	VQRDE.X	5.94	+0.46	6.00	6.30	1	472
30.00	VQRDF.X	2.80	+0.00	2.80	2.95	468	3,071
35.00	VQRDG.X	0.99	+0.06	0.90	1.00	535	8,316
40.00	VQRDH.X	0.35	+0.02	0.25	0.35	27	4,524
45.00	VQRDI.X	0.15	+0.05	0.10	0.20	32	5,106
50.00	VQRDJ.X	0.10	0.00	0.05	0.10	3	3,036

The Option chain (table) explained

1. Strike price: How much I'm willing to pay for the stock or sell the stock.

2. Symbol: of the option. Options, like stock, are assigned a symbol for ease of trading and identification. Each different strike price is a different option and therefore has a different symbol.

3. Last price: Last price at which the option was either bought or sold.

4. Change: Whether the option is up or down on today's last price as compared to yesterday's closing.

5. Bid: What I sell for. Think of it as wholesale and retail. When I sell, I get wholesale.

6. Ask: What I buy for. This is the retail price. When I buy, I buy at retail.

View By Expiration: Mar 07 | **Apr 07** | Jul 07 | Jan 08 | Jan 0

CALL OPTIONS   Expire at close Fri, Apr 20 2007

Strike	Symbol	Last	Chg	Bid	Ask	Vol	Open Int
15.00	VQRDC X	16.88	0.00	14.50	14.70	40	314
17.50	VQRDW X	20.70	0.00	12.30	12.50	0	20
20.00	VQRDD X	12.10	0.00	10.10	10.30	8	441
22.50	VQRDX X	11.70	0.00	8.00	8.20	6	237
25.00	VQRDE X	5.94	↓0.46	6.00	6.30	1	472
30.00	VQRDF X	2.80	↓0.08	2.80	2.95	468	3,071
35.00	VQRDG X	0.99	↓0.06	0.90	1.00	535	6,316
40.00	VQRDH X	0.35	↓0.02	0.25	0.35	27	4,524
45.00	VQRDI X	0.15	↓0.05	0.10	0.20	32	5,106
50.00	VQRDJ X	0.10	0.00	0.05	0.10	3	3,036
55.00	VQRDK X	0.05	↓0.10	N/A	0.10	60	1,346
60.00	VQRDL X	0.05	0.00	N/A	0.05	50	1,151

NOTE: There are always two price quotes in the market; a bid and an ask price. It's a rather irritating fact that the price I'd like to have, is not the price I'm going to get.

7. **Volume:** How many contracts were opened today.

8. **Open Interest:** How many contracts are open not counting today.

3 Tools needed to trade the market

As stated earlier (page 9), whether an expert or a beginner:

Everyone needs 3 tools to be successful in today's market. The observation that everyone needs three tools is important. But, it is absolutely useless if you are not given a clue as to what they are and where to find them. I am aware that any book including all the potential tools available to trade would be too heavy to lift. Chapters 3, 4, and 5 use specific tools that have worked for me. My criteria for selection are as follows:

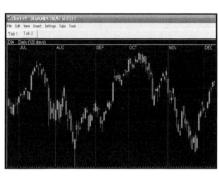

1. The resource I'm using is free or very inexpensive
2. The resource gives me buy/ sell signals, not general opinions
3. The resource has dignity. It does not promise unrealistic rates of return and it has an honest approach to the market

To review, I need:

–1. A Search Engine
•Find stocks that fit the strategy I'm applying (Covered Calls)

–2. A Charting Software
•No one should ever buy a stock without charting it
•Charting software should have a rich selection of technical indicators to assist in raising the probability of a successful trade.

- My charting software should provide easy access to a
    news feed to check for
        –Current news, if existing, about the stock being
          considered.
        –WHEN earnings announcements are
          forthcoming.

Do not make a trade if earnings on the stock comes out before the option expires.

–3. A Brokerage House

•No matter how good a "picker" I am, it does no good if I don't buy the stock (or short it, depending on the direction of the stock)

•Each investor should find a broker with whom he/she is comfortable, and open an account. Also, you ought not worry that you have to be right the first time you pick a broker.

This is important. If you find, after trading with a specific brokerage account that there are others offering services geared more to your specific needs, change. If your broker is your inept brother-in-law and you are afraid it will hurt his feelings if you switch, change anyway. Your broker needs to be able to service your account effectively and completely. You don't have to have warm and fuzzy feelings about him. If you need that, buy a puppy.

Chapter 3
Search Engines

One of the great dangers in the age of electronics is taking information from too many sources. Find a few search engines you like and stay with them. Sometimes there's a tendency to buy every new product making a claim that you are about to be given the secrets that the stock brokers or bankers or the Market "do not want you to know".

Some time ago, I came to the sobering conclusion that the stock brokers or bankers or market makers probably do not care what I know or don't know. It's the publishers of the new gizmo that don't want me to know something. And usually what they don't want me to know is that the new 100% fool-proof gizmo only works for about 5% of the people buying it, if at all.

Search engines help me wade through the basic qualifications of my selected strategy. In the case of covered calls, the search engine finds stocks that are trading from $10.00 to $50.00, have options, and return from 3% to 8% per month.

Just like about everything in life, there is no one single solution. Finally, one strategy may require a different search than another. A calls and puts search engine looks for entirely different characteristics in a stock behavior than a covered calls search engine.

Some great search engines that look for covered calls include:
- CoveredCalls.com
- Power Options (poweropt.com-a fee-based search, but perhaps the most powerful and complete search engine available)
- OptionsXpress.com

I've worked with or have an association with one or more officers of all of the web-sites listed above, so perhaps my opinion is somewhat tainted. I've also used their products and find them to be very effective. For me, a search engine has to

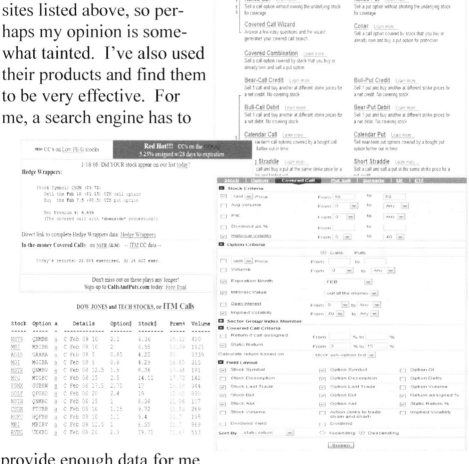

provide enough data for me to be able to make a definitive buy or no-buy decision (with a little extra homework) right now. Search engines that suggest purchase within the next 6 months or because the sector is strong, even though the stock is trending downward are of little use in my trading style. Like the late Flip Wilson, I have a membership in the church of "What's happening now".

Finding Covered Calls with CoveredCalls.com
A search engine is:

A computer program, newspaper, technical journal…
Any tool that helps the investor find one or more stocks with specific, in-common characteristics which, if bought or sold, would increase the chance of success in the market.

Usually search engines are thought to be electronic in nature. There are many search engines available on the Web. Coveredcalls.com is one search engine that can be very instrumental in increasing the chances of making a profit and reducing the amount of time needed to "find" covered calls.

Further, CoveredCalls.com is, as the name implies, focused on Covered Calls only. It does no other searches.

Among other things, it also gives advise on how to play Bollinger Bands with RSI.

Stock	Option	a	Details	Option$	Stock$	Prem%	Volume	OI	BB&RSI
RIGL	QRGLB	a	C Dec 07 10	0.7	8.26	8.47	26	1307	RIGL
CSIQ	GQALE	a	C Dec 07 25	2.05	24.59	8.34	1548	742	CSIQ
WCI	WCILA	a	C Dec 07 5	0.4	4.81	8.32	807	1748	WCI
MEDX	MWMLC	a	C Dec 07 15	0.95	13.35	7.12	3740	35525	MEDX
PMI	PMILW	a	C Dec 07 17.5	1.2	17.24	6.96	1694	1572	PMI
MTG	MTGLF	a	C Dec 0						
ABK	ABKLF	a	C Dec 0						
BONT	QHWLC	a	C Dec 0						
HOV	HOVLB	a	C Dec 0						
SVNT	UVPLD	a	C Dec 0						
BMRN	NURLF	a	C Dec 0						
RYL	RYLLY	a	C Dec 0						
SHFL	SFQLV	a	C Dec 0						
CRME	UXYLV	a	C Dec 0						
NBIX	UOTLC	a	C Dec 0						
WM	WMLD	a	C Dec 0						
HRB	HRBLD	a	C Dec 0						
PHM	PHMLV	a	C Dec 0						
SUF	SUFLA	a	C Dec 0						
THC	THCLI	a	C Dec 0						
SLXP	PQNLV	a	C Dec 0						
AMR	AMRLD	a	C Dec 0						
SA	SALF	a	C Dec 07 30	1.2	29.44	4.08	280	1529	SA

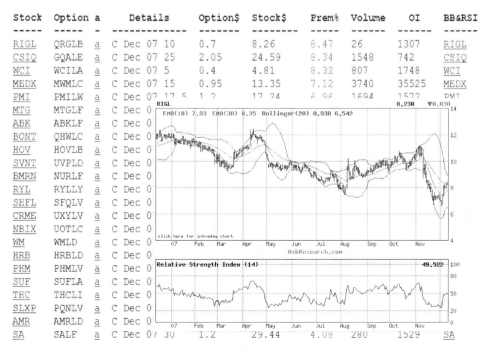

There is also a small primer on covered calls that is very helpful in understanding the play better.

As stated, Coveredcalls.com is a free website. Like most search engines, it does not presume to do my thinking for me. It finds potential covered call candidates. It is my responsibility to chart the stock, check the news and check for pending earnings announcements.

WARNING:
There is no attempt by Coveredcalls.com to screen out stocks trending downward. **If you trade into a downtrend, it's a kiss of death.**

1. Go to Coveredcalls.com

2. Click on 30 days.

   Coveredcalls.com now screens over 190,000 different option contracts.

Note that we are looking at December calls.
These option contracts expire in the month of December.

The date we preformed this search was December 11th. The
search engine doesn't look exactly for 30 days, It looks for the options expiring in the
current month. Still,
the search engine says
30 days. If I click on
60 days, it looks for
options expiring the
month following the
current month. A bit
of a semantic prob-
lem, but not serious.

Remember that options
expire on the 3rd Fri-
day of December.
That means there are
only 10 days left in
this option contract. If
we can get 3% for 10
days, we've done very
well. Especially if the
stock charts in an up-
ward or sideways
trend.

5% to 10% Calls for December

*** Data is updated DAILY...Data last updated 12/10/07 for NEXT business day ***
(Premium Percentages 5% to 10%)
Percentages are not on margin and are not "in-the-money"....why
Remind me how to read Bollinger Bands & RSI
a = Analysts' Recommendations

DOW JONES and TECH STOCKS, or ITM Calls

Stock	Option a	Details	Option$	Stock$	Prem$	Volume	OI	BB&RSI
RIGL	QRGLB a	C Dec 07 10	0.7	8.26	8.47	26	1307	RIGL
CSIQ	GQRLE a	C Dec 07 25	2.05	24.59	8.34	1540	742	CSIQ
WCI	WCILA a	C Dec 07 5	0.4	4.81	8.32	807	1748	WCI
MEDX	MWNLC a	C Dec 07 15	0.95	13.35	7.12	3740	35525	MEDX
PMI	PMILN a	C Dec 07 17.5	1.2	17.24	6.96	1694	1572	PMI
MTG	MTGLF a	C Dec 07 30	2.05	29.99	6.84	3147	4078	MTG
ABK	ABKLF a	C Dec 07 30	1.8	29.42	6.12	4664	17376	ABK

We are going to look at CSIQ because the price of the stock indi-
cates a stronger stock than RIGL, the stock above it.

WARNING: Always check the stock price and the option price at
current market prices. Coveredcalls.com's price quotes are end-of-
day quotes.

Quick Analysis: Looking at the second stock that was found by the search engine:

1. I could buy the stock CBIQ for $24.59.

2. I could sell the December 25.00 Options for $2.05

3. That's a profit of 8.3% and it can potentially re-occur each month. Also 8.3% is far above my minimum return requirement of 3% per month.

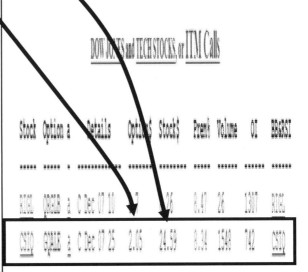

5% to 10% Calls for December

*** Data is updated DAILY...Data last updated 12/10/07 for NEXT business day ***

(Premium Percentages 5% to 10%)

Percentages are not on margin and are not "in-the-money"...why

Remind me how to read Bollinger Bands & RSI

a = Analysts' Recommendations

DOW JONES and TECH STOCKS or ITM Calls

Stock	Option a	Details	Option$	Stock$	Prem%	Volume	OI	BB&RSI
*****	*****	*	*********	*******	*******	*****	******	******	******
RTGI	QRSIB a	C Dec 07 10	.7	9.76	8.4	26	1077	RTGI
CSIQ	QQAIE a	C Dec 07 25	2.05	24.59	8.34	1598	742	CSIQ

34

STEP #1 Complete (Using a search engine)

Now we've found a stock using a search engine.
–It has options
–We are receiving more than 3% per month on the premium

After setting up this trade, on December 11th, I went back and charted the stock on the day of expiration. It closed at $27.45 (see the chart and window out take below). That means the market bought my stock away from me at $25.00. I received an extra $.41 because I bought the stock at $24.59. My premium was $2.05 + $.41 I made at the sale of the stock for a total of $2.46. The stock cost $24.59. Dividing $2.46 by $24.59 = 10%. for 10 days. Is this a great country or what?

If I put this into perspective and assume that I bought 1,000 shares of CSIQ that would mean I spent $24,590.00 for the stock. Then I could sell 10 contracts (100 shares per contract). I would receive $2,050.00 in my account. In 10 days, when my stock sold, I would receive another $410.00. With current interest rates, I could deposit $24,590 in a bank. In roughly 4 years, I'd have an additional $2,460.00. In the stock market I earned that much in 10 days.

Risk? Yes, there is risk, but if I am an informed stock market trader, and my winning trades are at or above 60%, it is a

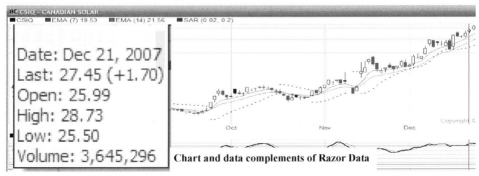

Date: Dec 21, 2007
Last: 27.45 (+1.70)
Open: 25.99
High: 28.73
Low: 25.50
Volume: 3,645,296

Chart and data complements of Razor Data

Chapter 4
Charting for successful trades

Two charting programs that are very good and are free are StockCharts.com and Big-charts.com. The problem is that they take a lot of "mousing around" to get them set up correctly. Once you get familiar with your

own personal likes and dislikes regarding a charting program, I'd suggest you shop around for some that might be more responsive to your own specific style of trading. Many brokers offer a charting module. Some are very powerful, and some need, in my opinion, more personality. Bigcharts.com is extremely helpful in that it has dividend,

earnings, and split indicators on its interactive charts. You can also apply, on a limited basis, technical indicators. StockCharts.com might be a little more flexible than Big-charts.com. but lacks the indicators for dividends, earnings and splits. As a sidebar, John Murphy, an advisor for Bigcharts.com is, in my opinion, one of the special people in the market. He's been my unwitting mentor for years. A great resource if you're looking for a steady voice in a sea of confusion.

Charts that need more personality, because I can discern nothing more than the very basics of the direction of the stock flow are like the one shown at the right. Again, charting like just about everything is a personal issue. Find what works best for you and stay with it.

Charting the stock, checking the news, and looking up earnings announcement dates is the 2nd step of my process for finding covered call plays.

The Library of Congress must be half full of books explaining how to chart. We'd like to keep it simple. Basically, the stock must be
–Trending slightly upward or
–At least basing in a sideways move.
–It CANNOT be trending down. Do not trade into a down trend. Did I say that already?

The key to success behind the covered calls strategies is largely dependent on picking a stock that has the right chart pattern.
We cannot overemphasize the importance of charting a stock..

Also, charting is very dependent on individual perception. One person's perfect chart may be another person's upset stomach. You may see a great trade and another person sees failure in the same chart.

Whatever your decision on when to make a covered call play I can unequivocally say that if you trade into a down trend, there's a huge chance you're going to lose. At the very least you will make considerably less money than if you wait until the trend turns up.

NO!

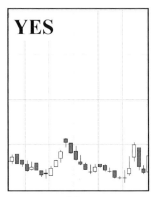
YES

YES

In the previous chapter, the search engine found the stock Canadian Solar (CSIQ). The stock costs $24.59 and the premium for the December 25c = $2.05.

$2.05/$24.59 = 8.3% for 12 days. 8.3% rate of return in 12 days is an extremely positive rate of return. Remember that this search was done on December 10. The options expire on December 21st.

Stock	Option	Details	Option $	Stock $	Prem%
CSIQ	GQALE	Dec 07 25	2.05	24.59	8.34

The chart below gives a positive picture of the direction of CSIQ. It may be argued that the stock is growing too fast and should be considered for a pure option play to capture more profit. For the time being, however, we'll keep it as a covered call play.

As you get more familiar with charting, you can apply technical indicators to aid in your decision to make or not to make a trade. Personally I like 4 indicators and they've served me well over the years.

They are

7 and 14 Exponential Moving Average combined
Support and Resistance
Full Stochastic 14,5,3
Trend Lines

These indicators are, by no means, all-inclusive. They work for me. You may find others that serve your trading style much better. Others to be considered include

Fibonacci Lines
Bollinger Bands
Relative Strength Index
Average True Range
DMI
...and the list goes on.

What I'd like to discourage is having too many indicators. Find 3 or 4 you like and stick with them. You can replace them as you find others more to your liking, but the operative word here is "replace". If you get more than 4 on your chart, you start to have sensory overload and soon you'll be unable to make a decision which is the very reason you employed the technical indicators in the first place...to help you make a decision.

At this juncture, we are simply looking for stocks that are trending slightly upward or basing sideways.

Stocks in a down trend are said to be experiencing 3 or more lower highs. Stocks in an uptrend demonstrate 3 or more higher lows.

Now the fun starts. How many days apart must the higher lows or the lower highs be? Unfortunately, much to the disappointment of my engineering friends, there is no exact answer. That's where I use moving averages to help. Since the strategy is covered calls, in an uptrend, I look for the 7 (or the smaller value moving average) day moving average to be on top of the 14 (or the greater value moving average) day moving average or I don't consider the higher lows to have existed long enough to have established a trend.

I also like the stochastic to be coming up off the 20 base line as opposed to going down from the 80 base line.

As you can see from the last part of October through it's breakout in mid-January, Sepracore provided ideal opportunities to make covered call trades.

41

An additional indicator:

Sometimes, much to my discomfort, my favorite indicators don't work. Nothing works all the time. If there were indicators that cast such a wide net as to work all the time, they would be too general in nature. They would get me, if at all, in the trade too late and out too early.

During those times when the market is extremely unpredictable, it's nice to have maybe one or two extra indicators if the one's you've been used to just are not working. Two that I've found to be very helpful are Bollinger Bands from John Bollinger and RSI from Wells Wilder. They work best when used together.

Generally, the accepted strategy as applied to covered calls is illustrated by the following table and accompanying stock chart. Coveredcalls.com provides an excellent primer on how to use Bollinger bands with Relative Strength Index (RSI) if you'd like additional information on this setup.

Stock Price touches the lower Bollinger Band and RSI is less than 30	A relative low in the stock price may have been reached and an upturn in stock price may occur in the near term	Buy the stock Sell OTM covered call

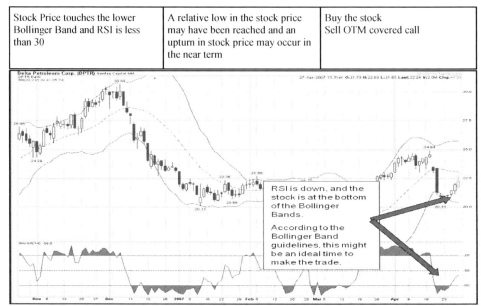

The second half of the charting requirement has nothing to do with charts at all. It has to do with checking the news...new information about the company itself. The news is not necessarily related to the charting process, but I always check the news right after I chart the stock.. I want to make sure there is no bad news about the company that might adversely affect the stock in the immediate future. This is often a tough call. Some companies can announce that they're not having a good quarter. This is bad news, right? Wrong. It turns out that the quarter was not as bad as was expected and the stock goes up 4 points. So when I check the news, I make sure that I trade the actual response of the market, not what I think the response should be. Fortunately this is an easy thing to do. Look at the stock chart. If it is trending up on the news release, it's good news, trending down, bad news.

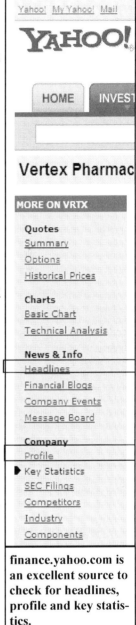

finance.yahoo.com is an excellent source to check for headlines, profile and key statistics.

Most importantly, don't hold a stock over earnings. Remember an option contract lasts until the 3rd Friday of the month. If a company plans to declare earnings before that Friday, don't go into the trade.
Unless you have an intimate relationship with the Chairman of the Board and know, without doubt that earnings and future guidance for the stock are going to beat the street, and you have an affidavit from the SEC authorizing you to engage in insider trading, don't hold over earnings.

The stock we've been working with is Canadian Solar. I ran a search on **CoveredCalls.com** to find the company. Then I charted the stock using **StockCharts.com** to make sure it was not in a down trend. Now I'm going to check the news using **finance.yahoo.com** to find out if there's anything I should be aware of which would make me not want to own the stock even though it is trending strongly to the upside. I hope the news will support my decision to buy the stock and sell the option. Using Yahoo to check for news I see that there is no

discernable bad news. To the contrary, this solar energy company from China seems poised to make great strides in the solar energy business.

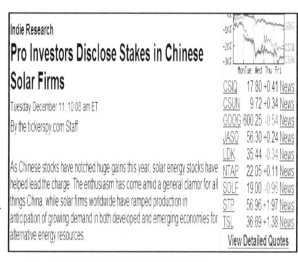

Now I need to check the earnings announcement date. One of the quickest ways to do this is to go to **earningswhispers.com**.

There are other websites offering earnings information, but sometimes the data is a little hard to find. Earnings Whispers gets right to the point.

Entering CSIQ into the "ticker lookup" box, I can see that CSIQ will declare

earnings on 2/13/2008, long after my options expire.

You do not have to jump around between websites if you have one that provides all your research data in one place. A few brokers provide all the information, charting capabilities and option tables in one easy-to-use website. Street Smart Pro from Charles Schwab is one.

OptionsXpress is a little less nimble when I mouse around the website but offers better search engines for covered calls, in my opinion. I also think TDAmeritrade, Fidelity Active Trader

What Has Been Done So Far

At this juncture a search engine has been selected to find potentially viable covered call plays. Specifically I was looking for a stock that was:

1. Basing sideways or trending upward
2. Had options
3. Returned > 3% on the option premium (the premium divided by the price of the stock)

Once a potential stock was isolated, I charted it and then checked the news to make sure:

1. I was aware of any potential news that might adversely or favorably affect the trend of the stock
2. I was not selling a call that expires after the earnings announcement

Below is an excerpt from the search engine generated by Coveredcalls.com. It is a partial option table and a good place to start to explain the fields in the table.

Stock	Option	Details	Option $	Stock $	Prem%
CSIQ	GQALE	Dec 07 25	2.05	24.59	8.34

Any option table or chain contains basically the same information.

Coveredcalls.com (CCC) displays less information than *finance.yahoo.com* illustrated earlier in the book. Nevertheless there is sufficient data to make a good basic decision whether to continue the analysis on one or more of the stocks and options found.

The Fields Explained:

| | 1 | | 2 | | 3 | | 4 | | 5 | | 6 |

Stock	Option	Details	Option $	Stock $	Prem%
CSIQ	GQALE	Dec 07 25	2.05	24.59	8.34

1. Stock Symbol
2. Option Symbol
3. Details (CCC) puts a lot of data in this field. There are 3 pieces of important information here:
    a. December = Month the option expires
    b. 07 = year the option expires
    c. 25 = strike price of the Call
4. Option $ is the premium for the option...the price I receive if I
    sell the option.
5. Stock $ is the price of the stock
6. Prem % stands for Premium Percent. It is the amount of percent I make on the trade. It is derived by dividing the price of the option ($2.05) by the cost of the stock ($24.59).

		Strike Price		Option Price		Stock Price	
Stock	Option	Details	Option$	Stock $	Prem%
CSIQ	GQALE	Dec 01 25	2.05	24.59	8.34

Here's the basis behind an option premium. Essentially when I buy a stock and sell the market the right to buy it away from me, I'm agreeing to hold my stock until the option expires. Remember I bought CSIQ at $24.59. I'm offering to sell it to any interested party for $25.00 (the strike price). At this point, no one wants to pay me $25.00 for a stock selling for $24.59 in the market. But there are many people willing to buy an option for the right to buy the stock at $25.00 if during the life of the option, the stock goes up in price to, say $28.00. Therein is the (derivative) basis for the options market. Traders buy the right (an option) to buy stock at fixed price ($25.00) before some future date. They believe the stock price will rise to some number above $25.00, say $28.00. If it does go above $25.00 at option expiration, they buy the stock from me for $25.00 and pocket the difference. The premium of $2.05 of $2.05 (circled above) is the price I receive for keeping my stock available through the life of the option and being willing to sell my stock for $25.00. It is mine to keep. Regardless of what happens to the stock, I do not have to give the premium back.

A stock can only do 3 things. Two of those, up or sideways, work well for a covered call strategy.

If a stock is above $25.00, on the day the option expires my stock will be purchased from me at $25.00. I'll receive the cash in my account and I get to keep, of course, the $2.05 premium I received for making it available for someone to buy during the life of the option.

If the stock goes sideways and closes on or around the price I paid for it, on the day the options expire, I keep my stock and determine if I want to sell another covered call for the next month.

Sometimes, against my best laid plans, a stock goes down. Unfortunately, no one has been able to consistently break any stock of this seeming whimsical and annoying habit.

If the stock goes down and I no longer wish to own it myself, I simply buy back the option I sold (it will be worth much less since time has passed and the value of the stock has gone down). Then I sell my stock, absorb the loss, and move on to my next trade.

There are a number of traders who espouse a repair strategy to avoid losing money when a trade goes against them. It involves buying back the option they sold and selling another that places them in a more advantageous trading position. While this is sometimes a viable approach, most of the time, it appears to me that they are trying to get back to just above break even and they're willing to take one or more additional months to do this. I think we ought not lose sight that time is money. I'd rather take a small loss on my current trade, find a better trade and pick up a profit on a new more profitable trade and absorb the loss by making more money faster. A personal opinion, of course.

Different strike price positions

- In the money calls (less than the price of the stock)
- At the money calls (same as the price of the stock)
- Out of the money calls (more than the price of the stock)

The standard procedure for covered calls is to buy a stock and **sell a call 1 strike price out of the money.** Since "out of the money" is not a phase used in normal day-to-day speech, it requires some additional explanation.

Below is an overview of strike prices which are in, at and out of the money. The following pages will combine these concepts with a full option table and present a clearer picture of how purchase the right option for a covered call play

Stock Price	Strike Price for call options	In, at or out of the money
	$15.00	In the money
	$17.50	In the money
$20.00	$20.00	At the money
	$22.50	Out of the money
	$25.00	Out of the Money

In-the-Money Options

To determine if an option is in the money, at the money, or out of the money, I must first check the price of the stock.

Symbol	Last	Time	Courtesy Razor Data	Change	Bid
CROX	29.89	2008-01-18 16:00:08		0.06	29.6

			Calls					Feb 2008
Ticker	Last	Change	Bid	Ask	Vol	Open Int.	Delta	Strike
CQJBD.X	10.3	+0.5	10.3	10.7	15	147	0.92	20.0
CQJBR.X	7.91	-0.09	8.2	8.5	2	136	0.89	22.5
CQJBE.X	6.3	0	6.2	6.5	221	932	0.77	25.0
CQJBF.X	3.2	-0.2	3.2	3.3	804	3943	0.55	30.0
CQJBG.X	1.5	-0.1	1.4	1.6	734	5136	0.33	35.0
CQJBH.X	0.6	-0.05	0.6	0.7	257	5874	0.16	40.0

Example:
–CROX, the stock, costs $29.89
An option with a strike price less than the price of the stock is considered "in-the-money.
In this case, the first strike price in-the-money is the $25.00 strike price. It is said to be "1 strike in-the-money". The $22.50 strike price is said to be "2 strikes in-the-money", and so on.

Out-of-the-Money Options

I have no idea if a stock is in, at, or out-of-the money without knowing the price of the stock.

When making a covered call play, I am looking for call options that are out of the money.

Symbol	Last	Time	Courtesy Razor Data				Change	Bid
CROX	29.89	2008-01-18 16:00:08					0.06	29.6
Calls							**Feb 2008**	
Ticker	Last	Change	Bid	Ask	Vol	Open Int.	Delta	Strike
CQJBD.X	10.3	+.5	10.3	10.7	15	147	0.92	20.0
CQJBR.X	7.91	-0.09	8.2	8.5	2	136	0.89	22.5
CQJBE.X	6.3	0	.2	6.5	221	932	0.77	25.0
CQJBF.X	3.2	-0.2	3.2	3.3	804	3943	0.55	30.0
CQJBG.X	1.5	-0.1	1.4	.6	734	5136	0.33	35.0
CQJBH.X	0.6	-0.05	0.6	0.	257	5874	0.16	40.0

Example:
–CROX, the stock, is holding at $29.89
An option with a strike price more than the price of the stock is considered "out-the-money.
In this case, the first strike price out-of-the-money is the $30.00 strike price. It is said to be "1 strike price out-of-the-money". The $35.00 strike price is said to be "2 strikes out-of-the-money", and so on.

At-the-Money Options

At-the-money options are a bit harder to find because that circumstance only exists when the stock price and the strike price are the same.

Symbol	Last	Time	Courtesy Razor Data					Change	Bid
CROX	30.00	2008-01-18 16:00:08						0.06	29.6

Calls								Feb 2008

Ticker	Last	Change	Bid	Ask	Vol	Open Int.	Delta	Strike
CQJBD.X	10.3	-0.5	10.3	10.7	15	147	0.92	20.0
CQJBR.X	7.91	-0.09	8.2	8.5	2	136	0.89	22.5
CQJBE.X	6.3	0	6.2	6.5	221	932	0.77	25.0
CQJBF.X	3.2	-0.2	3.2	3.3	804	3943	0.55	30.0
CQJBG.X	1.5	-0.1	1.4	1.6	734	5136	0.33	35.0
CQJBH.X	0.6	-0.05	0.6	0.7	257	5874	0.16	40.0

Example:
The price of the stock is now $30.00. The at-the-money strike price is the strike price that equals the price of the stock. So, the $30. 00 strike price is at-the-money.

There are a number of mentors, coaches, and lecturers who say the at-the-money strike price is the "closest" strike price to the price of the stock. Not so, according to the Options Industry Council.

At-The-Money
   A term that describes an option with a strike price that is equal to the current market price of the underlying stock

Which Option to sell?

This is a delicate issue. Fist fights in seminars across the nation break out over this question. (Ok, maybe not.) Hoping not to cause one, in this book I'll always sell 1 strike price out of the money.

•FIRST I must consider the price of the stock…
–Assume the stock I am considering is selling for $21.50
•SECOND I consider the first strike price out- of- the- money. In this example, the $22.50 strike price.
•THIRD I try to sell the most current month. If the premium for the current month is not equal to or greater than 3% but I already own the stock or I want to own the stock for investment purposes I can sell 2 or 3 months worth of premium.

To clear up any confusion let me clarify. If I own 100 shares of stock I can sell one call contract for any month I choose. What I cannot do is sell a contract for the current month and a contract for another month at the same time.

Usually, as mentioned earlier, it's more profitable to sell a contract for the current month than to sell one with more than one month's time.

–Often, I get asked "why am I even selling a call if the stock might go up?" Why don't I just hold the stock? Because it might not go up. I'm looking for the consistent cash flow. When I sell a call, I get money in my pocket from the "lease to own" aspect of the covered call.

Option Tables (Option Chains) have different values for each stock

An option table or option chain is like a supermarket for the various options available on a specific stock. There are many different options from which to choose.

The option table is a table showing the price of a specific options for a specific stock. Each different option has a different strike price and a different premium. The values of the options changes as the price of the stock changes. I can subscribe to a data feed, and pay a subscription price and get instantaneous updates or I can subscribe to a free data feed which usually has a 15-minute delay. Yahoo.com is a free data feed and also provides a fee-for-service date feed which is a real-time (instant) update.

If I am trying to conserve on costs, I'll take the 15-minute delay freebee. Prior to making the trade I can pull up a real-time on-line quote from my broker which often does not vary a great deal from the 15 minute-delay price quote.

CALL OPTIONS — Expire at close Fri, Mar 16, 2007

Strike	Symbol	Last	Chg	Bid	Ask	Vol	Open Int
27.50	SQXCY Y	3.30					
30.00	SQXC						
32.50	SQXCZ X	0.05					
35.00	SQXCG X	0.05					
37.50	SQXCU X	0.05					
40.00	SQXCH X	0.05					
42.50	SQXCV X	0.05					

Titanium Metals Corp. (TIE) — On Mar 9: 35.53 ↑0.35 (0.99%)

CALL OPTIONS — Expire at close Fri, Mar 16, 2007

Strike	Symbol	Last	Chg	Bid	Ask	Vol	Open Int
15.00	TIECC X	19.20	0.00	20.40	20.60	17	955
17.50	TIECW X	16.					
20.00							
22.50							
25.00	TIECE X	10.50					
30.00	TIECF X	5.60					
35.00	TIECG X	1.10					
40.00	TIECH X	0.10					
45.00	TIECL X	0.05					
50.00	TIXCJ X	0.03					
55.00	TIXCK X	0.05					
60.00	TIXCL X	0.05					
65.00	TIXCM X	0.05					
70.00	TIXCN X	0.10					
100.00	TIXCT X	0.05					

Microsoft Corp. (MSFT) — On Mar 9: 27.29 ↓0.03 (0.11%)

CALL OPTIONS — Expire at close Fri, Mar 16, 2007

Strike	Symbol	Last	Chg	Bid	Ask	Vol	Open Int
10.00	MQFCB X	17.80	0.00	17.25	17.35	56	432
12.50	MQFCV X	15.30	0.00	14.75	14.85	11	462
17.50	MQFCW X	9.87	0.00	9.75	9.85	10	696
20.00	MQFCD X	7.75	0.00	7.25	7.35	10	473
22.50	MSQCX X	4.65	↓0.75	4.75	4.85	135	702
25.00	MSQCJ X	2.38	↑0.01	2.31	2.35	646	14,542
27.50	MSQCY X	0.20	↓0.04	0.18	0.19	5,514	24,206
30.00	MSQCK X	0.02	↓0.01	0.01	0.02	2,236	52,636
32.50	MSQCZ X	0.01	0.00	N/A	0.01	15	25,137
35.00	MSQCL X	0.01	0.00	N/A	0.01	5	5,230
37.50	MSQCU X	0.02	0.00	N/A	0.01	5	65
45.00	MSQCI X	0.01	0.00	N/A	0.01	23	23

Chapter 5
Selecting a profitable option

I can sell a call option on any stock I own, previously purchased or on one I just purchased. However, it must have options. To make sure a stock has options, I can carry a list of the 3,000 +/- stocks for which the market makers make an option market. Keeping this list in my hip pocket, creates the impression that one half of my back side is distended. Another way is to simply look them up on finance.yahoo.com as illustrated earlier. I prefer the balanced backside look.

If my stock has options, I now wish to select the right option to sell.

The option guidelines are simple:
1. Current month
2. 3% rate of return
3. One strike price out of the money

There are a number of sources for option quotes in an option table. To eliminate me having to say "option chain" after I say option table, each time, just be aware that, for the purposes of this book, they are synonymous.

Quote services that are widely used and respected include:
- CBOE.com
- finance.yahoo.com
- smartmoney.com
- optionseducation.org

For this book, I'll use finance.yahoo.com. It is easy to read and free. It is, however on a 15 minute delay.

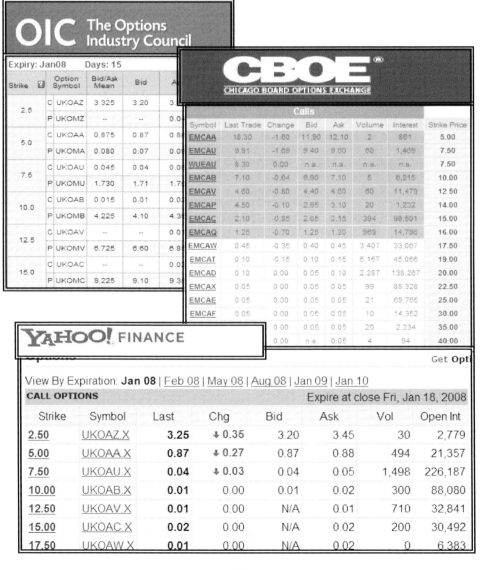

OIC The Options Industry Council

Expiry: Jan08   Days: 15

Strike		Option Symbol	Bid/Ask Mean	Bid	A
2.5	C	UKOAZ	3.325	3.20	3
	P	UKOMZ	--	--	0.0
5.0	C	UKOAA	0.875	0.87	0.8
	P	UKOMA	0.080	0.07	0.0
7.5	C	UKOAU	0.045	0.04	0.0
	P	UKOMU	1.730	1.71	1.7
10.0	C	UKOAB	0.015	0.01	0.0
	P	UKOMB	4.225	4.10	4.3
12.5	C	UKOAV	--	--	0.0
	P	UKOMV	6.725	6.60	6.8
15.0	C	UKOAC	--	--	0.0
	P	UKOMC	9.225	9.10	9.3

CBOE — CHICAGO BOARD OPTIONS EXCHANGE

			Calls				
Symbol	Last Trade	Change	Bid	Ask	Volume	Interest	Strike Price
EMCAA	18.30	-1.60	11.90	12.10	2	861	5.00
EMCAU	9.91	-1.69	9.40	9.60	60	1,469	7.50
WUEAU	8.30	0.00	n.a.	n.a.	n.a.	n.a.	7.50
EMCAB	7.10	-0.64	6.90	7.10	5	6,215	10.00
EMCAV	4.60	-0.80	4.40	4.60	60	11,479	12.50
EMCAP	4.50	-0.10	2.95	3.10	20	1,232	14.00
EMCAC	2.10	-0.35	2.05	2.15	394	98,501	15.00
EMCAQ	1.25	-0.70	1.25	1.30	969	14,796	16.00
EMCAW	0.45	-0.35	0.40	0.45	3,407	33,067	17.50
EMCAT	0.10	-0.15	0.10	0.15	6,167	45,066	19.00
EMCAD	0.10	0.00	0.05	0.10	2,287	138,267	20.00
EMCAX	0.05	0.00	0.05	0.05	99	88,328	22.50
EMCAE	0.05	0.00	0.05	0.05	21	69,765	25.00
EMCAF	0.05	0.00	0.05	0.05	10	14,352	30.00
		0.00	0.05	0.05	20	2,234	35.00
		0.00	n.a.	0.05	4	94	40.00

YAHOO! FINANCE

Get Opt

View By Expiration: **Jan 08** | Feb 08 | May 08 | Aug 08 | Jan 09 | Jan 10

CALL OPTIONS   Expire at close Fri, Jan 18, 2008

Strike	Symbol	Last	Chg	Bid	Ask	Vol	Open Int
2.50	UKOAZ.X	3.25	↓0.35	3.20	3.45	30	2,779
5.00	UKOAA.X	0.87	↓0.27	0.87	0.88	494	21,357
7.50	UKOAU.X	0.04	↓0.03	0.04	0.05	1,498	226,187
10.00	UKOAB.X	0.01	0.00	0.01	0.02	300	88,080
12.50	UKOAV.X	0.01	0.00	N/A	0.01	710	32,841
15.00	UKOAC.X	0.02	0.00	N/A	0.02	200	30,492
17.50	UKOAW.X	0.01	0.00	N/A	0.02	0	6,383

Two Quotes are better than one

Even though coveredcalls.com gives me an option quote, it is for one strike price per stock. I like to see more than that for a fuller picture of all the options for the month I'm considering. Some brokers have great option tables but they don't have a good charting program. And visa versa. I've been unable, at this point to find a perfect web site that provides a good search engine, a good charting program complete with news links and a good brokerage trading platform. Your experience many be different. In any case, until the "perfect" trading platform comes along, I'll use
finance.yahoo.com to find my option tables.

Coveredcalls.com's data is compiled at market close of the previous day. Prices from today's quote and yesterday's quote can be different. Actually, the price of the option changes shortly after the price of the stock changes so an option price change can happen any time of any day. In any case, just be

Delayed Quote from CoveredCalls.com

DOW JONES and TECH STOCKS, or ITM Calls

Stock	Option a	Details	Option$	Stock$	Prem*	Volume	OI	BB&RSI
TOA	TOADA a	C Apr 07 5	.45	4.66	9.66	162	50	TOA

Current Quote from Finance.yahoo.com

Symbol	Last	Time	Change	Bid	Ask	Open	High	Low	Close	Volume
TOA	4.66	16:31:44	-0.43	4.61	4.68	5.10	5.19	4.53	5.09	2633100

			Calls				Apr 2007				Puts				
Ticker	Last	Change	Bid	Ask	Vol	Open Int.	Delta	Strike	Ticker	Last	Change	Bid	Ask	Vol	Open Int.	Delta
TOADZ.X	0	0	1.9	2.35	0	0	1.00	2.5	TOAPZ.X	0.05	+0.05	0.05	0.15	170	0	-0.0
TOADA.X	0.40	-0.35	0.40	0.50	162	50	0.46	5.0	TOAPA.X	0.90	+0.35	0.85	0.90	258	618	-0.4

Finding and using the Yahoo option table

Go to finance.yahoo.com. Do not type in "www". The next screen appears. On the "investing" tab, click on "options".

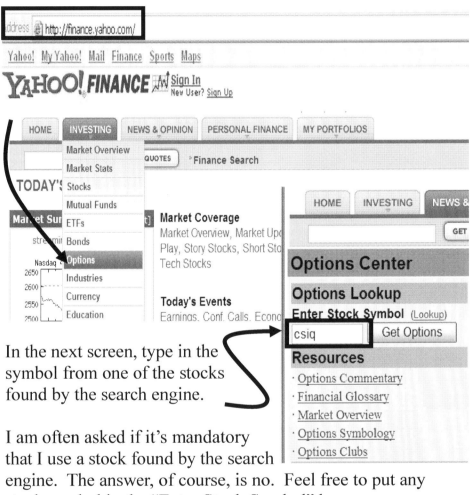

In the next screen, type in the symbol from one of the stocks found by the search engine.

I am often asked if it's mandatory that I use a stock found by the search engine. The answer, of course, is no. Feel free to put any stock symbol in the "Enter Stock Symbol" box.

Many people are pleasantly surprised to find that they can sell calls on stock they already own. If an option chain appears for the stock symbol typed in, the stock has options. It's that simple.

When I sell Options, I sell at the "Bid". Just like selling an automobile. The Salesman gives me the wholesale price for my car (the bid).

When I buy Options, I buy at the "Ask". Again, like buying a car. I pay retail.

In this example, I buy Canadian Solar Inc (CSIQ) for $27.79.

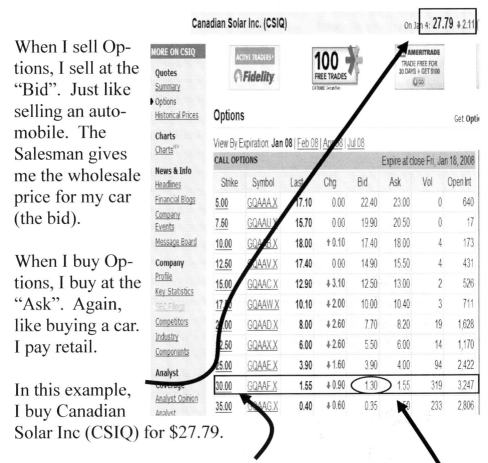

Canadian Solar Inc. (CSIQ)   On Jan 4: **27.79** ↓2.11

MORE ON CSIQ

Quotes
Summary
▶ Options
Historical Prices

Charts
Charts

News & Info
Headlines
Financial Blogs
Company Events
Message Board

Company
Profile
Key Statistics
SEC Filings
Competitors
Industry Components

Analyst
Coverage
Analyst Opinion
Analyst

Options   Get Opti

View By Expiration: **Jan 08** | Feb 08 | Apr 08 | Jul 08

CALL OPTIONS   Expire at close Fri, Jan 18, 2008

Strike	Symbol	Last	Chg	Bid	Ask	Vol	Open Int
5.00	GQAAA.X	17.10	0.00	22.40	23.00	0	640
7.50	GQAAU.X	15.70	0.00	19.90	20.50	0	17
10.00	GQABX	18.00	↑0.10	17.40	18.00	4	173
12.50	QAAV.X	17.40	0.00	14.90	15.50	4	431
15.00	GQAAC.X	12.90	↓3.10	12.50	13.00	2	526
17.50	GQAAW.X	10.10	↓2.00	10.00	10.40	3	711
20.00	GQAAD.X	8.00	↓2.60	7.70	8.20	19	1,628
22.50	GQAAX.X	6.00	↓2.60	5.50	6.00	14	1,170
25.00	GQAAE.X	3.90	↓1.60	3.90	4.00	94	2,422
30.00	GQAAF.X	1.55	↓0.90	1.30	1.55	319	3,247
35.00	GQAAG.X	0.40	↓0.60	0.35	.50	233	2,806

I then sell the market the right to by my stock away from me for $30.00...the first strike price out of the money.

The market pays me $1.30 for my commitment to hold my stock through January 18th. It is the bid price of the option

The option expires in 14 days. It is January 4th and the January options expire on January 18th.

The Market, must buy my stock, on or before the option expires on the 3rd Friday of January. That will only happen if, on the day the option expires, the stock is trading higher than $30.00 (my strike price). In that case, the market will pay me $30.00 for my stock and I will make an additional $2.21.

59

Remember it doesn't matter if the stock is trading for a much higher number than $30.00. I only get $30,00 because I agreed to sell it for that amount. Still, I make $1.30 for the commitment to hold my stock.

Here's the fun stuff: I paid $27.79 for the stock. I sold an option that expires in 14 days. I receive $1.30 for my option. $1.30/ $27.79 = 4.6% for 14 days. 4.6% for 14 days is a very good rate of return. Now I feel like the guy hawking knives on TV…"but wait, there's more". If the stock goes above $30.00, the market takes my stock and pays me $30.00. That's an additional $2.21. $2.21 + $1.30 = $3.51. $3.51/27.79 = 12.63% for 14 days. That is an even better rate of return.

Before I get too far afield jumping up and down at the prospect of a 12.63% rate of return let's look an order ticket for this trade.

An order ticket for the purchase of the stock and the sale of the option would look like this:

The price of the stock on today's market quote is $24.68. The option at the bid is going for $1.75.

So I buy 100 shares of stock at $24.68 for a total of $2.469.00 plus

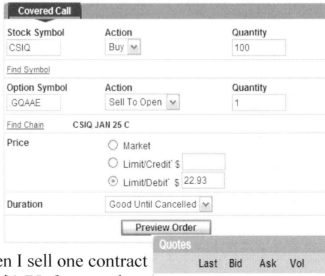

commissions. Then I sell one contract of Jan 25 calls for $1.75. for a total income of $175.00. That means that there is a net debit coming out of my account in the amount of $2,293.00 less commissions.

When the option expires in 14 days, if the stock is above $25.00, the market will buy it away from me for a price of $25.00. They take the stock and $25.00 per share is deposited in my account.

If the stock is below $25.00, the market will not buy it from me. They don't want to pay me $25.00 on a stock worth say $24.50. But I don't care. If I still like the stock and believe it to be in a trading range (which I do), I simply sell the February $25.00 options for approximately $3.50.

If the stock appears that it is dropping below its trading range I will simply sell the stock and walk away from the trade. Any money I made in premiums will hedge against the loss I sustained by the falling price of the stock.

What happens if the stock is falling and I want out of the trade and the option has not expired? This circumstance strikes fear into the hearts of brave traders. Many harbor the illusion that they cannot get out of the trade until the option expires. Not so! I simply buy my option back and sell my stock.

For example if the stock falls to $23.00 and I think it is going to fall still farther, I buy my January 25c back. Remember I sold it for $1.75. However since time has gone by and the stock has fallen in value, the price of the option will probably be worth about $.25. So, I buy it back for $.25. I sold it for $1.75 so I made $1.50 on the selling and buying of the option. Once I've bought my option back, I can sell my stock any time

I wish. The $1.50 I made hedges against the loss I sustained in the stock. I paid $24.68, I sold it for $23.00. I lost $1.63 on the stock, but I made $1.50 on the option. The net loss was $.63, not $1.63 that I would have lost if I had just bought and sold the stock. It is critical when I fill out the order form that I instruct the broker to buy back my option at market. Otherwise I will be "naked the call" and that is the riskiest trade in the market.

Fortunately, with new developments in the broker software, this really isn't a situation I need to worry about. Unless I have special permission from my broker, the software will not let me set up a trade where I am naked the call (don't have the underlying stock to cover the call).

An order ticket to sell the stock and buy back the option looks like the one above:

This order form says I wish to sell my stock (CSIQ) any time it drops below $23.00 (a contingent stop loss) and there is a contingent order to buy back my call options for the existing market price-at the "ask". This type of order is excellent protection against being trapped in the trade because I sold an option on the stock. It is not 100% fool proof but it's way ahead of second place. It also prevents me from being "naked the call". Said differently, a naked call is when I sell a call and have no underlying equity to back up my call position. In other words I do not own any stock. A number of advanced traders and very wealthy traders sell naked calls, but they live in a different strata than I do. I will swim with sharks, bungee jump and roller skate on the freeway. But I will not sell naked calls.

Check with your broker
There are over 900 (by one account) different brokers of good repute in the market. They all have a slightly different way of filling out an order ticket. Some are very similar, some are worlds apart. Further, not all brokers have the same flexibility in ordering options. There are still a few brokers who do not support option trading at all.

Whatever the case, please check with your broker as to the exact way he/she wishes you to fill out the order ticket. A number of brokers provide an excellent on-line tutorial.

PTI Securities out of Chicago uses the widely-accepted Interactive Broker platform. However, PTI Securities goes a step further than most. In addition to having a very inexpensive platform, they provide perhaps the best coaching and customer service in the business. At last report, every broker with PTI has been a previous floor trader. Having expertise on the floor, good customer service, and an inexpensive commission structure all in one brokerage house is almost unique in the market. And, no, I did not receive an override for this reference.

What happens if the stock goes above $25.00 before the option expires?

Rarely, will the stock be bought away from me before the option expires. It happens but only about 2% of the time. It usually happens when there is a trading imbalance (more options have been sold than the required number of stock shares exist necessary to cover the calls). The second reason is when the stock is above the strike price and a dividend is declared.

How much money does it really cost to buy the shares of stock and how much money do I really get when I sell the options?

When I sell a contract it controls 100 shares of stock. Prices in the option table are quoted on a "per share" basis. So when I get $1.30 per the option table on the previous page, it's really $1.30 x 100 or $130.00. Obviously I have to own 100 shares of stock or I cannot sell a contract.

I can, of course buy more than 100 shares of stock, but my purchase must be in lots of 100. So I can buy 100 shares of stock, 200 shares of stock, or as many as I feel would be a wise addition to my portfolio. I can only sell as many contracts as I have shares, divided by 100. For example. If I have 220 shares of a specific stock, I can only sell 2 contracts.

Also I can not sell more than one contract per 100 shares. For example, I can not sell 1 contract of January and 1 contract for February on the same 100 shares of stock.

Stop Loss Guidelines

There is a plethora of rules for setting stop losses. I've seen suggestions to set from 5%-2 1/2% below the purchase price. A very popular technique is to set a stop loss below yesterday's low stock price.

Covered calls, however, are different animals. My stop loss is lower because my stock break-even point is made lower by receiving a premium. So, without making a cast-in-concrete rule, my suggested stop loss is $1.00 below my break-even point. For example if I buy a stock for $25.00 and I sell a call for $2.00, my break even point is $23.00. Then I subtract $1.00 from the price of the break-even point. So my stop-loss is $22.00. That's it. Nothing fancy but it is very effective for me.

Start to Finish

To this point we've covered the broad scope of covered calls. The guidelines can be summarized very succinctly.
1. I employ a search engine to find a viable stock to purchase and then sell a covered call on it.
2. The stock I am looking for has the following characteristics:
    a. it is trending sideways or slightly upward
    b. the company is not going to announce earnings during the time the option is valid.
    c. there is no bad news that might create a cloud in the foreseeable future.
3. The option I sell:
    a. is for the current month.
    b. generates a minimum of 3% premium when divided by the price of the stock.
    c. is one strike price out of the money
4. I set a stop loss of $1.00 below my break-even point.

Observation: The language of the market is certainly a special language. It is not the Lingua Franca of the street. In this basic guide to covered calls I've attempted to make an introduction and provide the basis for making good out-of-the-money trades using the covered call strategy.

If you do nothing further to deepen your education, the principles I've gone over will serve you well making out-of-the-money trades. If you chose to go on...to become aware of different strategies where you can make a great deal more money, albeit not as consistently, visit *__Turbotrainer.com.__* They are continually adding their own instructional programs as well as sponsoring a library of proven educational vehicles from other authors. *TradersLibrary com* is also an excellent resource for books and other training material.

Chapter 6:
The Whole Process

After having learned the necessary elements of the market jargon for covered calls, I've reached a point where I can start the whole process of setting up a covered call trade.

You may remember that the first thing I do is employee a search engine to find covered calls. I am looking for a stock that is:

a. Basing sideways or trending slightly upward
b. In an upward trend
c. Has no bad news or pending earnings report in the period of time I plan to sell the option.

CoveredCalls.com

Free data for covered call investing

The search engine I am going to use is CoveredCalls.com. It is free. Its search algorithms however, do not consider the direction the stock is trading. So I could get all excited about good returns only to find the stock is trending downward. I have learned this rule the hard way: **Do not trade a stock in a downtrend.** When I visit the website, I am going to look for February Covered Calls since the current date is January 10th and there are only a few days left in January's options. The premiums for the January calls will be quite small since there are just a few days left before the January options expire. Remember the more time there is in an option, the more money it is worth. Typing coveredcalls.com into the internet address field takes me to the website.

I scroll down on the home page and since I am looking for February, but there is still some time left in January, I click on 60 days. I know it's not 60 days. To be exact it's 37 days, but the machine counts 30 days in a month regardless of the actual dates.

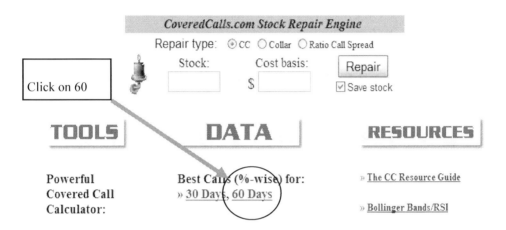

The partial results of the search engine are impressive. At first glance it would appear that I can get up to 18.84% rate of return for 37 days. This is where the wheels fall off the train for

Stock	Option	a	Details	Option$	Stock$	Prem%	Volume	OI	BB&RSI
NSTR	QNMBB	a	C Feb 08 10	1.5	7.96	18.04	171	640	NSTR
MBI	MBIBC	a	C Feb 08 15	2.55	14.11	18.07	1960	2496	MBI
ADLR	UAHBA	a	C Feb 08 5	0.65	4.23	15.37	2762	5487	ADLR
ZGEN	GZUBV	a	C Feb 08 12.5	1.8	11.99	15.01	37	862	ZGEN
CSUN	FTUBV	a	C Feb 08 12.5	1.65	12.16	13.57	210	996	CSUN
PMI	PMIBB	a	C Feb 08 10	1.1	8.89	12.37	345	485	PMI
HOKU	HQFBV	a	C Feb 08 12.5	1.4	11.42	12.26	139	2231	HOKU
RZ	RZBW	a	C Feb 08 17.5	2.05	16.81	12.2	221	387	RZ
CROX	CQJBF	a	C Feb 08 30	3.6	29.7	12.12	929	3430	CROX
AMD	AMDBI	a	C Feb 08 6	0.72	5.96	12.08	10142	5010	AMD

many people. Because of the monster rate of return (18.84% in 37 days is equivalent to 183% annually) they quickly buy the stock, sell the call and then watch as their stock tanks. They fail to chart the stock and fail to check the news.

Remember, don't trade into a downtrend and don't buy a stock that has pending news which might adversely affect the stock.

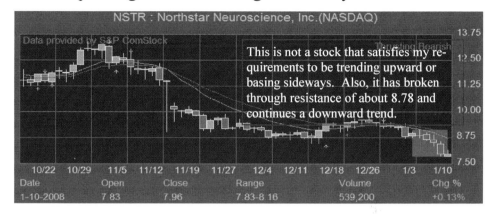

Look at a chart of the first stock in the list, NSTR and you get an idea of the danger of buying stocks just because the premium is attractive. However, the fact that the search engine finds some stocks that are "dogs" (going the wrong way) does not render the search invalid.

On the contrary any search engine helps a great deal to save time and often it finds stocks that I have not considered or never heard of. A good search engine is like having a very effective administrative assistant who wades through 190,000 different option contracts every day and finds a few that are potential covered call candidates. Once the search engine

gives me something to work with, I do a little homework. I chart the stock and check the news. Pulling up a chart on ZGEN, the 4th stock found in the search, I see that it was in a down trend. But in the last 4 days, it has reversed and is

moving back upward. It has support at or around the $10.50-$11.00 range. I really like the pattern of ZGEN. I need to try and find out why it is trading up. I look to the latest news on the stock which usually gives me the reason. Stocks just don't suddenly start to trend upward. News about it is read by enough of us, we find it favorable, and a buying movement starts.

One of the better news sources is *finance.yahoo.com.* To use their services, I need an internet connection. On the internet, in the appropriate URL Box, I type in the Yahoo address listed above.

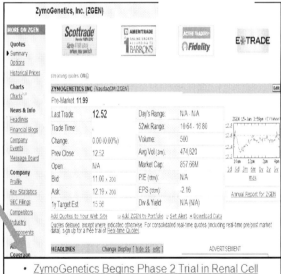

When the yahoo website comes up, I type the symbol in the space provided and click on

"GET QUOTES". Yahoo returns with a specific profile about the pertinent perform-ance of the stock in question. Scrolling down the page to "Headlines" I click on the latest news release.
The news headline expands and gives me additional in-formation about the banner headline.

Press Release   Source: ZymoGenetics, Inc.

ZymoGenetics Begins Phase 2 Trial in Renal Cell Cancer Evaluating IL-21 Combined with Nexavar(R)

Tuesday January 8, 6:00 am ET

SEATTLE--(BUSINESS WIRE)--ZymoGenetics, Inc. (NASDAQ:ZGEN - News) today announced that the company has initiated Phase 2 testing of Interleukin 21 (IL-21) in combination with Nexavar® (sorafenib) tablets in patients with advanced renal cell cancer. The Phase 2 study is part of a Phase 1/2 clinical trial and will examine patients treated with the maximum tolerated dose identified in the recently completed Phase 1 dose escalation phase.

ZGEN has just initiated Phase 2 testing. I am reasonably sure these Phase 2 tests will last from 3 months to perhaps 10 months. It is subjective, and no one knows for sure, but I think 3 months is a safe bet. This is more than sufficient time to make a covered call play.

Although the news seems favorable to me, I always re-check the chart to make sure the Market thinks it's good information.

If, after the announcement, the stock starts an uptrend, the Market thought it was good news and the stock will reflect the beginning of an uptrend or a continuation of one. If the Mar-ket did not like the news, the stock will also reflect the market opinion and start a down trend or continue one. Expert after expert in the Market will tell you "the Market is always right". What I think does not matter. Follow the Market. As illus-trated earlier, ZGEN was in an uptrend, albeit a short one. The uptrend was why I went scrambling after a news release in the first place.

					Strike Price	Pre-mium	Stock Price	% Return			
ZGEN	GZUBV	a	C	Feb 08	12.5	1.8	11.99	15.01	87	862	ZGEN

Rechecking the results of the "CoveredCall.com" (previous page) search engine I see I may receive $1.80 premium on a stock closing at $11.99...a very respectable 15% (monthly) rate of return. This satisfies all the requirements for making a covered call trade. It might be a bit risky because it's a drug stock, but that's also what drives the premium up so high (volatility) and gives me great returns (15%).

Check Earnings! Please be sure to check the earnings date. "Earnings" is another way to spell volatility. A stock may surprise on earnings to the upside and tank, or surprise to the downside and go through the roof. It may stay the same price regardless of earnings. Adding to the confusion is the "g" word: "guidance". If earnings are up but guidance for the future quarter is not positive, look for the stock to run to the basement.

Without additional supporting examples, I hope to convince you not to hold over earnings. There are those market mavens who've made a science of trading over earnings and do it well. They are a breed apart. If you are one of them, please call me. I'll buy your lunch and plane tickct if you'll but visit my office and share your infallible secrets.

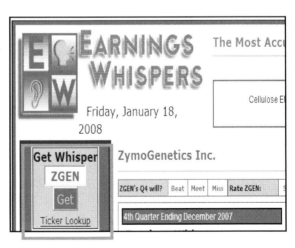

To find earnings announcements that are company specific, we need to go to a website with an earnings calendar. One site mentioned in this book already is: *http://biz.yahoo.com/research/earncal/today.html.* If you prefer Yahoo, for earnings announcement dates, use the address I

that comes up when I enter the correct address. I then type in the stock symbol in the box under "Get Whisper".

I see, from the results of the query regarding earnings that ZGEN will not announce until March. Since my options expire the 3rd Friday of February, I am safely inside the date for the announcement.

Earlier in the book 3 tools necessary for making a trade were illustrated.
1. Search Engine
2. Charting Program
    a. News Locator
    b. Earnings Calendar
3. Brokerage Firm

So far, the first two requirements have been satisfied on ZGEN. Now I need to establish a brokerage account if I do not have one or open my existing account to make a trade.

Also, earlier in the book, a rather forceful pitch was made for paper trading. If you take paper trading lightly, you are wasting your time. It needs to be a serious activity. Proven guidelines for successful paper trading include the following points:
1. Start with a limited amount, say $50,000. If you don't have that much to start with, it's ok. But you need about $50,000 in paper money to make multiple practice trades and get into the swing of things.
2. Before you invest, know your entry point, your exit point (for profit) and your stop loss.
3. Keep track of every trade you make. Keep a journal. When your trades are profitable, write why you think so and when they are not, write that down as well.
4. Do not invest real money until you are trading correctly about 65%-70% of the time and you are profitable on paper.

Everyone needs a practice trade account. It doesn't matter if you're an experienced trader of 20 years or a beginner. From time to time, we all lose our edge. That's the time to go back to paper trading until you are back to winning 65% or more of the time.

The website *CBOE.com* has a virtual trading package. It is free. If you don't have one, The CBOE Virtual Trade module works well. On your internet URL (URL stands for Uniform Resource Locator) page, type in CBOE.com and hit "enter".

Click on "Trading Tools". A drop-down menu appears. Click on "Virtual Trade Tool".

This is a partial picture of the next screen that appears on your computer.

I suspect nothing is ever really free, as in "you receive and you are not asked to provide something first". In this case, I have to provide the

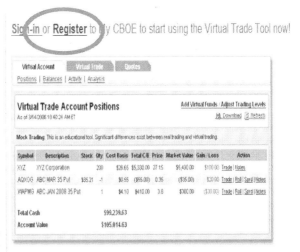

CBOE with my email address and a few other tidbits of information. I click on "Register", fill in the requested information, establish a user name and password and I can now paper trade.

Clicking on the "Virtual Trade" tab brings up the following menu (partial picture). Click on "Covered Call".

This is a blank order ticket for a covered call. To place an order in the market, I must, of course, establish a brokerage account. All brokers have some form or another of an order ticket. Unfortunately they are not all the same. The order ticket to the right is a good example of an order ticket. It is simple, all the data needed to place an order is on one page and the fields are clearly labeled.

The multiple fields behind an order ticket. There are 2 fields on the order ticket that require additional explanation. When buying stock, the order ticket is fairly simple. It is either a "buy" order or a "sell" order. It is the same with an option. The phrases are just a little different.

When buying an option contract, I "buy to open". But with covered calls I am not a buyer of the contract, I am a seller. So I *sell to open.*
I have filled out this order ticket

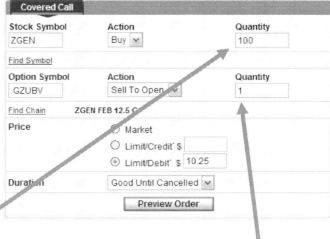

to buy 100 shares of ZGEN and sell 1 February $12.50 Call contract.

At the time this order was placed, ZGEN was selling for $12.00 at the "ask".

The February $12.50 calls were being sold at $1.75 per contract share ($175.00 per contract).

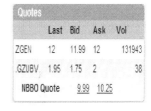

That means if I bought the stock for $12.00 and sold a call against my position, $10.25 would come out of my account. I would now own 100 shares of ZGEN and I would have sold the market the right to buy my stock at $12.50

Note: Finding the right option symbol can be a difficult task. The CBOE makes it easy. Remember it was the February 12.50 calls I wish to sell. I type in the stock symbol (ZGEN) in the option symbol window (shown above on the order ticket, but expanded here on an outtake. Clicking on "find chain" points the program to the option chains or option tables.

Once the order ticket has been filled out, I click [Preview Order] on at the bottom of the order ticket. A summary of my order appears. This is an excellent time to carefully read the data on the preview screen to make sure the order I want to place is, in fact, the order I did place. If I made a mistake or decide not to

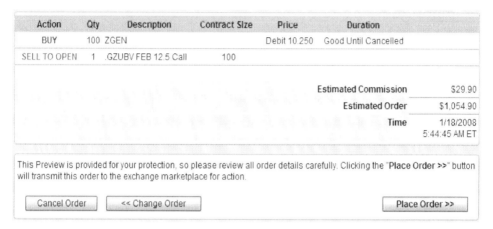

Action	Qty	Description	Contract Size	Price	Duration
BUY	100	ZGEN		Debit 10.250	Good Until Cancelled
SELL TO OPEN	1	.GZUBV FEB 12.5 Call	100		

Estimated Commission	$29.90
Estimated Order	$1,054.90
Time	1/18/2008 5:44:45 AM ET

This Preview is provided for your protection, so please review all order details carefully. Clicking the "Place Order >>" button will transmit this order to the exchange marketplace for action.

[Cancel Order]   [<< Change Order]   [Place Order >>]

place the order, I simply cancel the order or change the order. If I am still comfortable with the order, then I click on "place order", seen at the bottom of the summary ticket.

My covered call order now goes to market. It stays in a open status until it is filled. I know when it is filled because the little "open box" under the "Status" line changes to a green color and the word "filled" replaces "open".

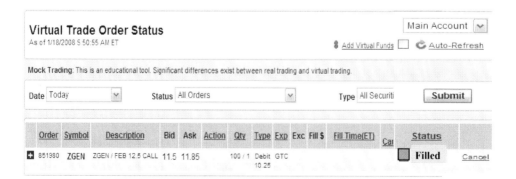

Virtual Trade Order Status
As of 1/18/2008 5:50:55 AM ET

$ Add Virtual Funds ☐ ↻ Auto-Refresh

Mock Trading: This is an educational tool. Significant differences exist between real trading and virtual trading.

Date [Today ▼]   Status [All Orders ▼]   Type [All Securiti]   [Submit]

Order	Symbol	Description	Bid	Ask	Action	Qty	Type	Exp	Exc	Fill $	Fill Time(ET)	Car	Status	
➕ 851980	ZGEN	ZGEN / FEB 12.5 CALL	11.5	11.85		100 / 1	Debit 10.25	GTC					■ Filled	Cancel

Placing a stop loss on ZGEN:

Setting a stop loss amount is somewhat of a subjective figure. For some stocks a stop loss fairly close to a purchase entry point works well because the stock is not a big mover. For a more volatile stock, a stop loss that is too tight might get me stopped out of the trade prematurely. For covered calls, I like to set my stop $1.00 below my break even point. For example, if the stock cost $37.00 and I received $2.00 for the option premium, then my stop loss would be $37.00- $2.00 = $35.00-$1.00 = $34.00. If the stock is a less-expensive stock i.e. $15.00 or lower, then I reduce the $1.00 to $.50. To get out of the trade, I sell the stock. And I "sold to open" the option. To get out of the option, I close the contract by issuing a "buy to close" order.

The stop loss point for ZGEN is calculated as follows:

Cost of the stock	$12.00
Premium received for selling the call	- 1.75
Stop loss is $.50 below the break even	- .50
Stop Loss:	$9.75

The stop loss for ZGEN takes two order tickets because a covered call stop loss order is a contingent order. The second part to set the stop loss would be filled out as follows:

If ZGEN's price falls to $9.75 or less,
1. Sell the stock.
2. Buy to close the option @ market.

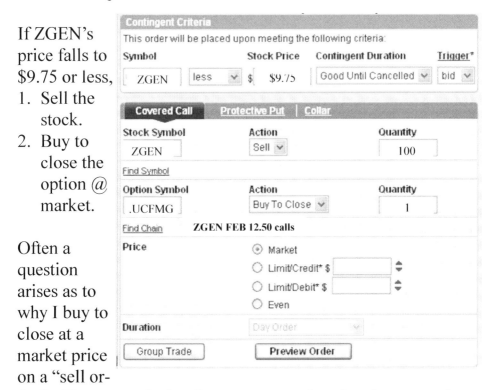

Often a question arises as to why I buy to close at a market price on a "sell order". The reason is that I must assume that time has passed since I bought ZGEN. It's price has dropped from $12.00 to $9.75. The two factors, passage of time, and reduction of price seriously reduce the price of the option. It is probably worth about $.25. But since I cannot project the price of the option, I have to sell it at a market price.

A general observation about filling out order tickets:
There are probably 3-4 ways to fill out an order ticket for a covered call. No one way is "correct". The best order is one that fills the quickest for the best price. Each broker uses a slightly different order ticket format. Please check with your broker for the way he or she feels is best. The above

examples are just that; examples. They are absolutely not absolute.

Very general guidelines on how to set an order up
I do have some general guidelines as to how to set an order up. They are as follows:

I set up a buy or sell order as a limit order and it is a day-only order. I set up a stop loss order as a market order and it is a good 'til cancelled order (GTC).

Logic trumps Rules:
If logic flies in the face of the rules, go with logic. For example, I once bought some contracts on QualComm. Overnight the price doubled. When I saw the new price the next day, I placed a sell order at a limit price. Unfortunately the option went down as fast as it went up. I lost a large portion of my profit because I did not change the sell order from a limit price to a market price. Each time I placed an order to sell at a limit equal to the current price, the stock was moving down too quickly for my order to fill. Had I placed my sell order at the market, I would have made a much larger profit.

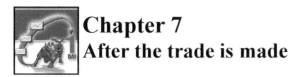

Chapter 7
After the trade is made

As stated earlier, a stock can only do three things. It can go up, down or sideways.

Here's what happens to my position in ZGEN in each of those three circumstances.

The day of reckoning is the day the option expires. In this case the 3rd Friday of February.

The stock goes above my strike price of $12.50

Remember I bought the stock for $12.00. I also promised to sell my stock to the market for the price of $12.50 (the option contract) even though the stock might go higher to perhaps $15.00. The market gives me $1.75 (premium) for the option I sold. That is mine to keep regardless of the price of the stock. Also, I receive the $1.75 in my account the day after I sold the contract. I can reinvest that amount if I wish or just take it out and spend it.

On the Monday following the day the option expires, the market deposits $12.50 per share in my account and I no longer own the stock. I make another $.50 on the deal. I made $1.75 on the option, $.50 on the sale of the stock for a total of $2.25. Dividing $2.25 by $12.00, I made 18.75% on the trade not counting the cost of commissions.

The stock stays relatively flat

If the stock stays at or around my purchase price of $12.00 when the option expires, the market does not want to pay me

$12.50. I still own the stock. I received $1.75 for the premium on the option I sold. I keep the $1.75 of course. I made $1.75 divided by $12.00 or 14% on the trade. If I still like the stock, on Monday following the expiration of the option, I sell the March $12.50 calls hopefully for near the same price I sold the February $12.50 calls. Almost all the time, the price for the option premium will not be the same each month. There are 5 factors that go into determining the price of the option. They are always changing and probably are never the same at the beginning of each month. So I might get $1.65 or $1.85 for the March $12.50 covered calls. If the volatility of the stock is down, I might only get $1.00. As long as I can get more than 3% return on my money each month, I am very comfortable. That is about 36% per year and it definitely pays the bills in South Dakota.

The price of the stock goes below my stop loss

You may remember that I set my stop loss on ZGEN at $9.75. If, at any time during the life of the option contract, ZGEN falls to or below $9.75, my stop loss kicks in. It sells ZGEN for $9.75 (or whatever it can get once the stop loss triggers). Note: The stock might fall right through my stop loss to maybe $9.00. And the price fell so quickly that the broker was unable to sell my stock at $9.75. It will be sold whenever it stops long enough to execute the sale. It might be at $9.75 or it might be $9.00. Remember that when the stock hits $9.75, (market order) the stop loss will be triggered.

Then when the stock is sold, the February $12.50 calls will be "bought to close" for pennies on the dollar. If the stock falls in value, so does the option. That works to my advantage. Remember I sold the option for $1.75. It is now worth hypothetically $.15. So I made $1.60 on the option. Although I lost

Chapter 8:
Summary and Conclusion

When first entering the market, there are challenges of learning a new vocabulary and new business concepts. For me there was also the excitement of the possibility of making an obscene amount of money. Much to my disappointment, there was not gold on the ground, ready for the picking. Trading is hard work. But it is rewarding when understood.

The market suffers fools poorly. The disciplined are rewarded. Back testing and paper trading should become your new best friends. The market also keeps a dear school (old English for "damn hard"). It continually surprises experts, does things which are totally unpredictable and defies consistent analysis. It is because it is built on historical performance, but more importantly, emotion. Fear and greed are the norm. Historical performance is a distant third. No one can correctly chart the first two.

If my personal experience is any measuring stick as a reality check for those just starting out, I have to do about 10 paper trades before I get comfortable with any specific strategy and can determine if it fits my personality. Also, I don't even consider a strategy unless it back tests successfully. I am aware that back testing has it's drawbacks. Still I'd sooner work with a strategy that back tests successfully over one that has not worked yet...but it might. And yes, I am writing a book on "testing strategies correctly".

I also found that I learn better when I trade with someone who is also trading or at least a trader. From time to time, I need to talk to some other upright walking carbon based human being.

My computer does not have a winsome personality. When I trade by myself for very long, I am in poor company.

To expand my trading experiences, I often attend workshops and webinars focusing on market subjects. Unfortunately, in my opinion, most, not all, are quite expensive and teach too much too fast. Workshops that cost a small portion of the national debt seem to be more about making the workshop sponsor money and less about teaching me the subject material. Bad PA systems, hard-to-read and hard-to-understand Power-Point presentations are the norm.

For a long time, we've been looking for a workshop company that taught one-day workshops which were simple, short, effective and inexpensive. We wanted to find an educational program that built on itself. One where you could take a basic class and then take an advanced class if you wanted. **However, it was not necessary to take the advanced class to understand the basic class you just took.** Finally if you took one class, we thought it would be nice to have learned enough to trade. Some workshops teach just enough to not quite be able to trade.

To our discomfort, there always seems to be someone who's last name ends in a vowel selling me more workshops in the middle of the one I was attending. (No offense to my Italian friends.) In some workshops, the pressure to buy more is palpable and intense.

We couldn't find anyone offering inexpensive, complete 1-day workshops. So we created our own. It is an educational system (***Turbotrainer.com***) which has a common thread running through it's entire educational fabric.

Strategies have to be proven effective through back testing or we won't teach them.

In the workshop, we show you the results of the back tests for the strategies we're about to learn. Just like us, if you're not excited about the strategy, you won't be interested in it. We really like the ones that make money.

We teach two basic workshops. We teach two intermediate workshops and two advanced workshops (six different workshops). You can take one, get good at the material and become a successful trader with that strategy. You don't have to come back. If you want to learn another strategy, come see us. It won't cost you the price of a second car.

We do request that you attend the basic strategy classes before moving to the more advanced levels. Each of our workshops is one day only. For those who prefer not to travel to a workshop destination, we have webinars. They are 2 hours long and there are 3 sessions, usually spread across 1 week's period of time.

We have an open forum website. If you have questions, you

can email us. We respond in 24 hours. Each week we send out 3 trading opportunities using one or more of the strategies we teach in our workshops.   There is a fee for the website. Currently, the monthly subscription is $19.99.

We have DVDs that support the material we teach. Everything we offer costs money, but our products and our workshops/ webinars are not expensive.

Our goal is to teach
       Effectively
       Inexpensively
       Quickly

If this philosophy is appealing to you, please look us up on the web at *TurboTrainer.com* and thank you for reading my book.

P. M. Batty

INDEX

Made in the USA